Hand Tools for Woodworkers

Principles & Techniques

Hand Tools for Woodworkers

Principles & Techniques

Robert Wearing

Sterling Publishing Co., Inc.
New York

All drawings and photographs by the author except where
otherwise acknowledged.

Library of Congress Cataloging-in-Publication Data Available

10 9 8 7 6 5 4 3 2 1

Published 1997 by Sterling Publishing Company, Inc.
387 Park Avenue South, New York, N.Y. 10016
Originally published in Great Britain by BT Batsford Ltd
© 1996 by Robert Wearing
Distributed in Canada by Sterling Publishing
c/o Canadian Manda Group, One Atlantic Avenue, Suite 105
Toronto, Ontario, Canada M6K 3E7
Printed and bound in Singapore
All rights reserved

Sterling ISBN 0–8069–9578–5

Acknowledgements

I appreciate the help given in supplying some of the illustrations by Record Marples, Stanley and Eclipse Tools and by the Editor of *The Woodworker* magazine in permitting me to re-use material previously published there.

Contents

Introduction

In spite of the development over the years of all types of power tools, the principles and techniques of using hand tools remain at the very heart of woodworking. Although power tools enable you to work more quickly and cheaply, they rarely produce the kind of result obtained from using hand tools. For example, the power planer cannot match the finish of good hand planing, nor can machine-made dovetails compare with well-spaced and hand-cut dovetails.

Inevitably in a book of this size decisions as to what information to include had to be made. I have omitted numerous tools whose wooden forms have been superseded by metal and whose production has virtually ceased. These are really for the collector rather than the worker at the bench. The impact of the small power router has been enormous; it is now economically priced, well within the range even of many amateur workers, and consequently a number of the hand tools it replaces have been omitted.

Increasing numbers of adults, both men and women, find pleasure in working wood, quite apart from any financial needs. More and more houses now have garages, providing reasonable workshop facilities. Yet for so many people the only means of acquiring information is by either a two hour, once-a-week evening class, if one is accessible, or from books. It is hoped that this book will supply much of the essential woodworking information and start amateurs and possibly young apprentices on the right course.

Robert Wearing, 1996

Sharpening Edge Tools

All the edge tools are sharpened in much the same way although, of course, there are some individual differences. There are two main stages. The first is grinding, the putting on of the basic bevel (Fig 1.1a). The second is honing, sometimes called sharpening, which is the putting on of a sharp edge by means of a second bevel that is very small and fine (Fig 1.1b).

The grinding process was formerly carried out on large natural stones, which ran vertically in a trough of water, turned by hand, foot or later by electricity. This is now seldom the method of either the amateur or the professional craftsman. A recent development has been the small, horizontally-running water-cooled stone, a smaller version of professional oil-cooled stones. These very much fill a need, being economical in both cost and space. Suitable guides and toolholders guarantee success with minimal skill. New models are constantly appearing.

High-speed grinders, intended primarily for engineering, are commonly used. They are seldom wider than 1 in. (25 mm). A useful diameter is 6 in. (150 mm). The greatest care must be taken not to overheat the tool as this destroys the hardness. Frequent dipping-out in water is necessary.

The cycle of a cutting edge (Fig 1.2) follows this pattern: when bought, the edge has been ground only, so it is not fit for use. It is then honed, putting on a second fine bevel and making the tool usable. Later honings increase the angle of the honing bevel,

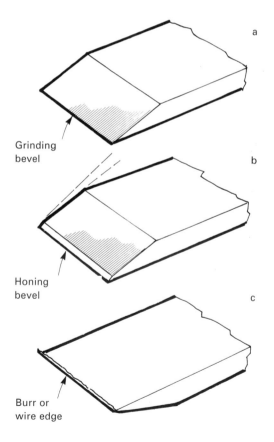

a

Grinding bevel

b

Honing bevel

c

Burr or wire edge

Fig 1.1

and also its area. Eventually the angle becomes so large that sharpness is lost and time is wasted in honing. The tool must then be ground back to its original bevel and the cycle begun again. Where good and convenient grinding facilities are available it is best to grind almost every time, the time spent on both grinding and honing being negligible.

Sharpening is easier with a honing guide (see Fig 1.4). There should be no indignity in using one of these. It makes a first-class job, reduces the amount of grinding and is particularly useful on narrow edges or edges which have to remain absolutely square.

Honing

Honing can be carried out on the traditional oilstone or on that relatively recent arrival, the Japanese water stone. Oilstones can be man-made or natural. Popular and economically priced man-made stones are the "India" by Norton in the fine and medium grades, or the Carborundum. The commonly accepted size for a bench stone is 1 x 2 x 8 in. (25 x 50 x 200 mm). Natural stones, such as the Arkansas and the Washita, produce very fine edges, but they are both slow-cutting and very expensive.

The stone should be housed in a wooden box, which is nowadays built up rather than cut from the

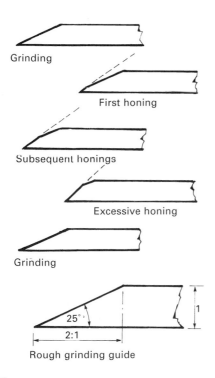

Grinding

First honing

Subsequent honings

Excessive honing

Grinding

25° 2:1 1

Rough grinding guide

Fig 1.2

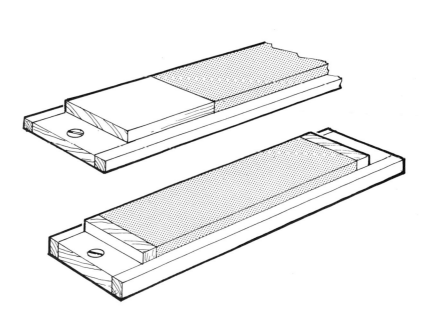

Fig 1.3 An oilstone box with lid of similar construction. Behind, an extended wood block for use with a honing device.

solid. A small end grain block at each end permits the full length of the stone to be used (Fig 1.3). Water stones must be kept wet. A narrow plastic freezer box makes a good container with an old squeezy bottle for the water. Water stones are quite soft, which makes them unsuitable for community workshops. Their cleanliness is an advantage, making them a good choice for the single woodworker.

As stones wear hollow they can be rubbed flat on a sheet of plate glass. For oilstones, use water and aluminium oxide lapping compound by Carborundum, which is available as coarse, medium and fine, to suit the particular oilstone. For water stones, use wet and dry abrasive paper, working from a coarse to the finer grits.

Having oiled or wet the stone, place the tool on, slowly lifting the handle until the bevel is flat on the surface. This is the position when the oil or water oozes out under the cutting edge. Raise the tool minutely. This is the honing position. You can use a honing guide (Fig 1.4) to help you find this position if you wish. Hone back and forth in this

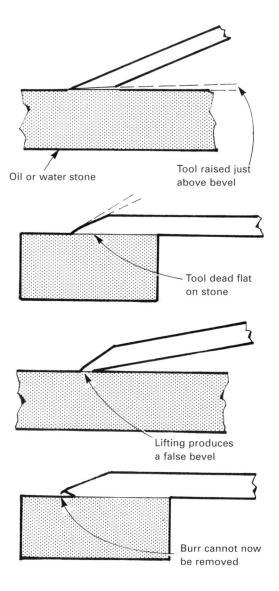

Oil or water stone

Tool raised just above bevel

Tool dead flat on stone

Lifting produces a false bevel

Burr cannot now be removed

Fig 1.4 A honing guide, stepped to take chisels or plane blades.

Fig 1.5

manner until the finest burr or wire edge can be seen along the entire edge. Reverse the tool and lay it dead flat on the stone – this is vitally important. Hone this way until the wire edge bends upward and repeat both the processes for a few strokes until the wire edge falls off. It can finally be cleared by stroking the edge through a piece of end grain wood, preferably not hand-held. The edge can be finished by stropping on leather glued to a wood strip and treated with fine valve-grinding paste, obtainable from a service station. The flat side of the tool must stay completely flat. Any trace of a bevel developing on the flat side makes it impossible to remove the wire edge without further increasing the false bevel.

This is the general method for sharpening most chisels and the square cutters of rabbet and shoulder planes. Variations of the method will be described under the individual tools.

Simple devices such as that shown in Fig 1.6, in addition to the honing guide (see Fig 1.4) already discussed, are very useful when sharpening. Fig 1.6 shows a device which helps to maintain accurately the grinding angle of a chisel when using a high

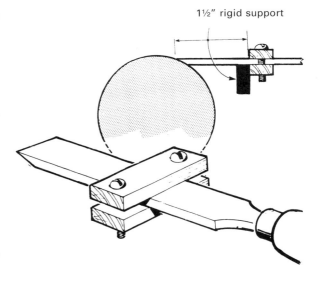

1½" rigid support

Fig 1.6

speed wheel. The tool must be dipped frequently into water. Overheating will destroy the temper and so the tool will not retain its edge.

Planes and Planing

Bench Planes

Discounting wooden planes, of which there is now a limited production and no general interest, there are three fully adjustable bench planes in cast iron.

The jack plane

With cutter widths of 2 and 2⅜ in., and lengths 14 and 15 in., this general purpose plane (Fig 2.1a) is mainly used to prepare components to size. Its cutter is sharpened to a gentle curve, ensuring the corners do not dig in and cause a step in the planed surface.

Fig 2.1a The jack plane.

The smoothing plane

(See Fig 2.1b.) This is made with cutter widths of 1¾, 2 and 2⅜ in., and lengths of 8, 9 and 10 in. respectively. The 2⅜ in. smoothing plane is favored by joiners, the 2 in. by cabinet makers, while the 1¾ in. suits youngsters, beginners and anyone working on smaller, finer work. It should be used in the final stages of work for removing negligible thickness. To avoid leaving a shallow fluted surface, it is sharpened virtually straight and square with just the corners eased away.

Fig 2.1b The smoothing plane.

The trying plane

(See Fig 2.1c.) With a cutter of 2⅜ or 2⅝ in. and a length of 22 in. this is, as the name originally meant,

Fig 2.1c The trying plane.

a truing plane. The greater length ensures more accurate planing of edges for jointing (hence its alternative name, "jointer") or large flat surfaces. For surface work, sharpen the blade like the smoother. For edges and use on the shooting board (see pages 119-21), it is sharpened quite straight and square, so it is a good idea to have two blades. A less common model is the fore or panel plane which is 18 in. long with a 2⅜ in. cutter.

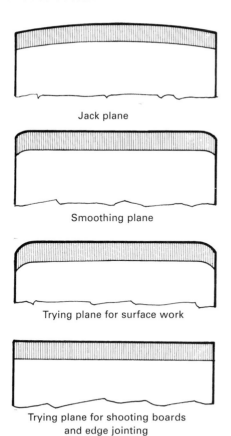

Jack plane

Smoothing plane

Trying plane for surface work

Trying plane for shooting boards and edge jointing

Fig 2.2 Grinding forms for plane irons.

Plane nomenclature

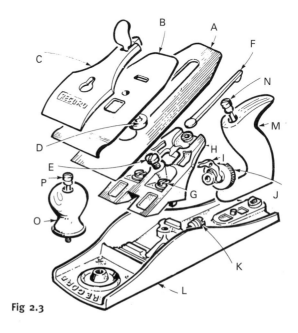

Fig 2.3

A-Blade	I-Y Lever
B-Cap iron	J-Cutter adjusting wheel
C-Lever cap	K-Frog adjusting screw
D-Cap iron screw	L-Body
E-Lever cap screw	M-Handle
F-Lateral lever	N-Nut and screw for handle
G-Frog screw	O-Knob
H-Frog	P-Nut and screw for knob

The wood jack plane

Almost the sole survivor of the family of wooden planes, this still has a following, remaining a firm favorite with a few serious woodworkers. However, since most schools have discontinued using them and are equipped with metal planes, a generation has emerged having no experience of the wooden jack, so like other wooden planes, it may well be doomed. Its claimed advantages are that it is almost indestructible and runs sweeter on the wood. (This latter is debatable when the iron plane is used with an oilpad.) Its critics cite the less convenient method of adjustment (by hammer), the length of time required to grind and sharpen the thick blade, the lack of a comfortable front grip and the handle set high above the work. To this add also the occasional planing true of the sole and the less frequent re-mouthing. Planing narrow edges wears the sole in the middle, making this truing-up necessary. Cut is increased by striking the blade and is decreased by striking the top of the fore part of the body. Better models had a striking button let in at this point.

Adjusting and using the plane

The first and least often used adjustment is the size of mouth. With the blade removed, the two frog

screws can be slackened and the frog or bed can now be moved back and forth with the adjusting screw. After adjusting, re-tighten the frog screws. A larger mouth permits rapid removal of wood with a coarse cut but a poor finish. A fine or close mouth permits only a fine shaving but gives a good finish. For a start, set a jack plane's mouth to about $\frac{1}{32}$ in. (1 mm) and a smoothing and try plane to $\frac{1}{64}$ in. (0.5 mm) or less. Attempting too fine a mouth causes clogging but will not be alone in creating this effect.

The cut, that is, the thickness of shaving removed, is controlled by the brass adjusting nut operating the "Y" lever which in turn operates in a slot in the cap iron, to which the blade is attached. Moving the nut clockwise increases the cut. After reducing the cut, the last adjustment must be a clockwise one to take up the slack in the mechanism. Naturally, a fine shaving produces a superior finish to a coarse one and two fine shavings involve less effort than one thick one.

The last adjustment is done with the lateral lever (see Fig 2.5), to prevent one side of the blade "digging in." The stud on the lateral lever must engage in the slot of the blade. This must always be checked when assembling the plane. The lever cap screw is commonly kept too tight. When correctly tight it should be just possible with the fingers, not the lateral lever, to move the blade slightly sideways.

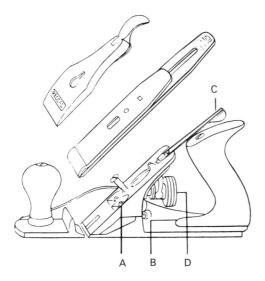

Fig 2.4 Metal plane adjustments. A and B for the mouth; C the lateral blade movement. D controls depth of cut.

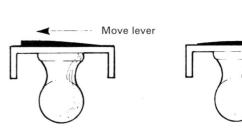

Move lever

Fig 2.5 Lateral adjustment.

To simplify, the function of the cap iron is to destroy the strength of the shaving and so reduce tearing. A fine finishing cut demands a close-set cap iron. For coarser, quicker work set the cap iron further back. Too close a cap iron combined with too fine a mouth will result in clogging. Guidelines for initial setting of the cap iron (Fig 2.6) are as follows:

- Rough preliminary work: 1⁄16 – 1⁄32 in. (1 – 1.5 mm)
- Finishing work: 1⁄64 in. (0.5 mm)
- Hardwoods with difficult grain: as close as possible without clogging

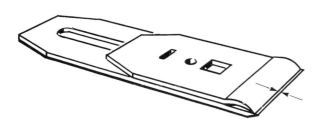

Fig 2.6 Setting of the cap iron.

Having pre-set the mouth and the cap iron, the plane can be made ready for use. Sight along the sole of the plane, and with the lateral lever, bring the blade symmetrical to the sole. Next withdraw the blade fully. Grip in the vise a piece of softwood, say ¾ x 3 x 12 in. (20 x 75 x 300 mm) with its edge uppermost. Start planing, slowly turning the brass adjusting nut until the first fine shaving results. This must be a very fine shaving. Stop here and adjust the lateral lever until this first shaving comes from the middle of the blade and not from either corner. Now you can apply the required amount of cut. This lateral adjustment should stay until the blade is removed or is accidentally knocked out of place.

It will be obvious now why the often-repeated advice (derived from the days of wooden planes) of laying the plane on its side when it is not in use is quite unsound. Far from protecting the plane, it can often result in upsetting the carefully adjusted lateral setting. A far better method of protecting it from knocks and scrapes is to park the plane on a wood strip covered with lightly-oiled felt or carpet. Doing this has the triple advantage of not disturbing the setting, lightly lubricating the sole and contributing to rust prevention.

Fig 2.7 Stance.

On this same edge, practice planing, aiming with each successive stroke to obtain a full-length, full-width shaving. Begin by settling the front of the plane well, i.e., ahead of the blade. Push forward until you feel the catch of blade, pause momentarily, and then push without taking a swing at it. At the commencement of the stroke it is very important to exert firm downward pressure on the front handle. A beginner trying this for the first time may need help to settle the front of the plane as shown in Fig 2.9a. The rear hand should be used merely to propel the plane forward. At the end of the stroke downward pressure is transferred to the rear handle while the front hand maintains forward motion. In the middle of the stroke, forward and downward pressure should be equally distributed between both the front and the rear hand. You should aim to stand with your feet in a position which you will find comfortable both at the commencement of the stroke and at the

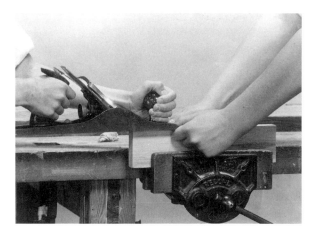

Fig 2.9a Assisting a beginner to settle the front of the plane.

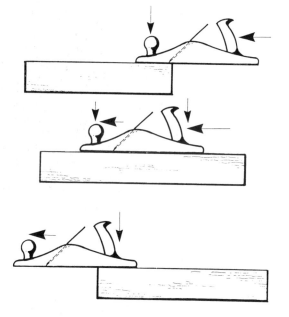

Fig 2.8 Hand pressure, when planing.

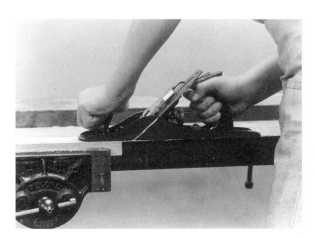

Fig 2.9b Start of stroke, downward pressure on front.

end of it. The correct stance for planing is shown in Fig 2.7 while the right way of applying hand pressure during the planing process is illustrated in Fig 2.8 and also in Fig 2.9b and c.

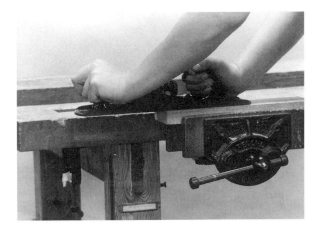

Fig 2.9c End of stroke. Note the downward pressure on the rear handle.

Fig 2.9d Edge grip, with the fingers used to form a fence.

When small pieces of wood are ripped out, producing a rough surface, this is called tearing. There are several possible cures for tearing which are listed below:

- Plane in the reverse direction
- Sharpen the blade
- Take a finer cut
- Set the cap-iron closer
- Set the mouth closer

Any one of the above suggestions, or a combination of any of them, should eventually provide you with a solution to the problem.

Preparing components to size

Before starting a project of any description it is first necessary to prepare each of your components to size. This involves two distinct processes – facing and edging.

Care and accuracy at this stage are necessary if you are to produce work of quality and are doubly important when making joints.

Facing

In preparing components to size, the first stage is to produce and test one true flat face. This is nowadays called the true face but was formerly referred to as the face side. The operation is known as facing.

With a jack plane, first plane off the dirt and roughness from one larger face. Set the cut fine and endeavor to plane the surface hollow. Take nothing from the ends. When the plane refuses to cut any further, plane from end to end, working systematically from side to side. As soon as you obtain continuous full length shavings, stop and test the surface.

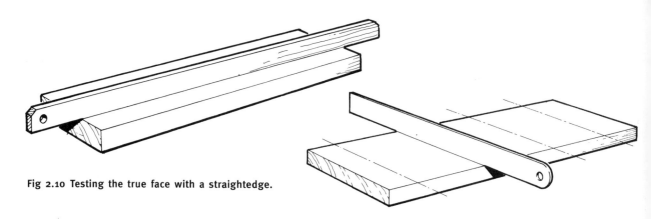

Fig 2.10 Testing the true face with a straightedge.

Fig 2.11 Testing the true face for flatness.

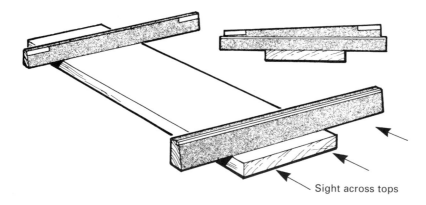

Sight across tops

Fig 2.12 Testing a true face with winding strips. Inset: a view showing a board in twist.

Tests for a true face

1   Is it flat in length? Test in several places with a straightedge longer than the work (Fig 2.10).
2   Is it flat in width? Test in places with a straightedge or rule longer than the width (Fig 2.11).
3   Is it in "twist"? Test with winding strips (Fig 2.12).

Correct an untrue face by taking fine shavings from the high spots, being careful that in correcting for one test, the other two are not upset. When all three tests are satisfied, mark with the face mark as shown in Fig 2.14.

Edging

The next stage is to produce an edge exactly square (i.e., at right angles) to this true face. This process is called edging. With a fine cut, first hollow the edge, taking nothing from the extreme ends, until the plane will cut no more. Now plane through from end to end until a full-length, full-width shaving results. Stop at this point and test for accuracy.

Tests for a true edge

1   Is it flat in length? Test with a straightedge longer than the work.
2   Is it flat in width? (a full width shaving should make this so). Test with a rule in several places.
3   Is it square to the face? Test with a try square along the edge. The stock of the try square must always be against the true face (Fig 2.13).

When these tests are satisfied, mark the edge, the mark coinciding with the face mark as shown in Fig 2.14.

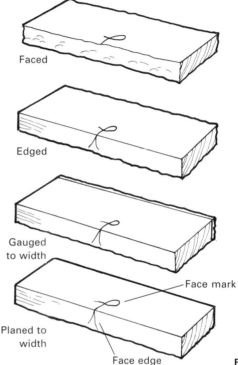

Faced

Edged

Gauged to width

Planed to width

Face mark

Face edge

Fig 2.14

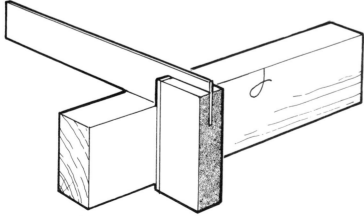

Fig 2.13 Testing the true edge.

Correcting an untrue edge

The jack plane cutter is sharpened to a slight curve, so it follows that while shavings from the middle are of uniform thickness, shavings from either side of the plane have a thick and a thin edge.

If one side of the wood is high, do not tilt the plane as this will produce a second surface. Instead, slide the plane over to the high side, keeping the sole flat on the existing surface, and plane full length shavings. These shavings, with a thick and thin side, will gradually bring the edge down. Test frequently for squareness. To produce finally to size, gauge the required width (see page 56) from the true edge and plane to the gauge mark. Then gauge it to thickness from the true face and again plane to the gauge line. These two operations can be done in either order. The gauge makes a V groove. When planing, half of this V is removed (see Fig 2.15). Removing the mark completely produces an undersized component so, if the remaining half of the gauge mark looks unsightly, ignore it. Later it will either be concealed or lost in a molding, in the bevel or in the final clean-up.

Planing end grain

Planing straight through the end grain produces tear-out, i.e., the breaking away of the end fibers. This

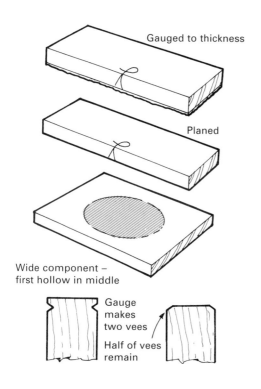

Gauged to thickness

Planed

Wide component –
first hollow in middle

Gauge makes two vees

Half of vees remain

Fig 2.15

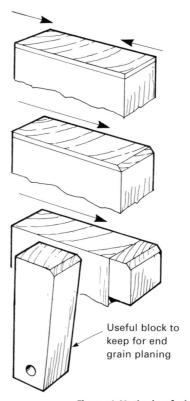

Useful block to keep for end grain planing

Fig 2.16 Methods of planing end grain.

can be avoided (as shown in Fig 2.16) by:

- Planing to the middle from each end
- Chiselling off a bevel in the waste
- Clamping or gluing on a bevelled block

Edge jointing

The technique of planing an edge has already been described. In making an edge joint the two joining edges are prepared in this way, being straight, flat and at right angles to the true face.

Grip one of the boards in the vise and stand the second one on top of it, testing first with a straightedge that the jointed boards will be flat (Fig 2.17). When you have found this to be correct, push very gently with an index finger on one corner. If the top board pivots, then one board is high at the pivoting spot and can be corrected (Fig 2.18). If the top board falls off, then either the joint is correct or is hollow (Fig 2.19). You can identify hollowness by looking through the joint into a strong light. Now that synthetic glues have largely replaced natural glues, most joints are clamped rather than rubbed. A clamped joint will permit very slight hollowness in the middle. The rule used to be that a very thin worn penny could just slip in at the middle of a six-foot joint.

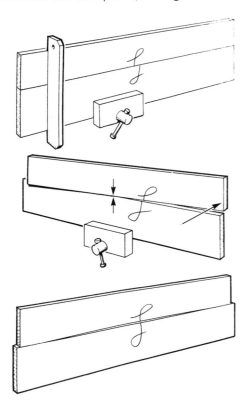

Fig 2.17 Edge jointing test for flatness.

Fig 2.18 Edge jointing. Pivoting will reveal high spot.

Fig 2.19 Edge jointing. Top board will not pivot but will show daylight and fall off.

Specialist planes

The vast collection of specialist planes which once filled so much space in the woodworker's tool chest is now largely extinct. A few such planes remain, however, which in a modern form are still useful:

The rabbet plane

This exists in two forms (Fig 2.20). The first is the Record 078 Duplex Rabbet and Fillister (and its Stanley counterpart), which has precision screw adjustment of cut. It also has a fence and a spur which can be brought into use as required when working along the grain on difficult lumber, or across the grain. A depth stop is also fitted.

The other version, the Record 010 and 0101/2, (and the Stanley equivalent) has a fine mouth and a close-set cap iron. It gives a good finish even on difficult woods. This makes it highly suitable for fielding panels. With no fence, it works along a clamped-on batten or from a groove cut previously by plow plane, power router or circular saw. When cutting rabbets, some pre-planning is necessary, particularly if using the fixed mouth planes, to ensure that the plane works along and not against the grain.

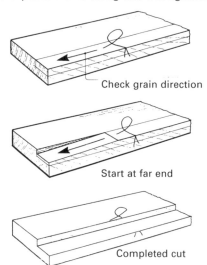

Check grain direction

Start at far end

Completed cut

Fig 2.21 Planing a rabbet.

Fig 2.20 Rabbet planes.

Fig 2.22 Shoulder planes.

The shoulder plane

The shoulder plane is in fact a special form of rabbet plane. At present two forms exist – the Record and the Stanley (Fig 2.22). Designed with a low angle, especially for planing end grain, the main purpose of this plane is the planing of the shoulders of mortise and tenon joints. Narrow shoulders should, of course, fit from the saw but they will occasionally require correction. Wide shoulders, however, will always require planing. The work is generally clamped to the bench and the plane used on its side.

In addition, the shoulder plane will cut small rabbets. It is particularly useful on difficult woods and can be used to work small ovolo molding.

The hand router

At the time of writing, this is manufactured only by Stanley. Two models are available: the standard full-sized one and a miniature version (Fig 2.23). Despite the rapid development in power routing there is still a place for these tools, which easily complete a small job before the electric router can even be set up. The most common task of the router is cutting across the grain housings for shelves and partitions, often

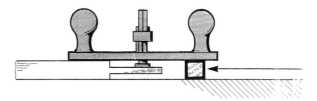

Fig 2.24 Truing a tenon with a hand router.

Fig 2.25 The Stanley hand router in operation leveling a housing on the right.

after saw cuts have been made. It can also be conveniently used to cut recesses for locks, hinges and fittings, and for inlaid features.

Though craftsmen are reluctant to admit it, occasionally tenons and bridle joints are cut over-thick. The router is by far the best tool to correct this fault. It is far more accurate than paring with a chisel. To keep the router level, an offcut of the same thickness as the job is either clamped alongside, or better still, screwed to the router sole utilising an existing hole.

These modern routers have cranked cutters, which must be kept very sharp since much of the work will be across the grain. The bevel is on top

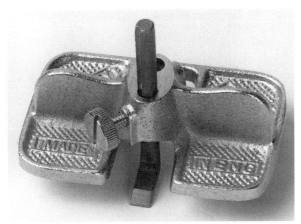

Fig 2.23 The Stanley miniature router.

and must not be allowed to grow stubby. The sharpening, generally with a flat stone slip, follows normal methods, though is rather inconvenient. The sole of the cutter, like the back of any other cutting edge, must stay flat with no trace of a bevel forming there.

Unavoidably, there is a certain amount of slack in the mechanism so after a cut has been completed, adjustment is made with the router standing in the cut. If it is held up in the air while the adjustment is made, then as the locking collar is released, the blade will drop, giving a greater increase in cut than was anticipated.

Unlike the rabbet and plow planes, it is not feasible to fit a depth stop. A considerable amount of adjustment and re-adjustment can be avoided if a cut is taken from all the housings in turn, then the cut increased and all the housings given this cut, repeating until the final depth is reached.

The plow

The modern all-metal plow plane (see Fig 2.26) has a fine screw adjustment of cut, an adjustable fence, depth stop and interchangeable cutters. As well as standard imperial sized cutters, from ⅛ in. upwards,

Fig 2.26 A modern plow plane.

metric cutters are available for use with millimeter-sized plywood. The small size of metal plow plane should not be despised. It performs well, its only limitation being the range of cutters it will accept.

Grooves are plowed almost always along the grain so, again in early planing, grain direction should be observed so that wherever possible the plow cuts with the grain. The plow lacks spurs, so on difficult wood it is best that the sides of the groove are first gauged with cutting gauges, set with their bevels inwards.

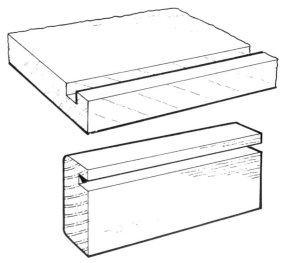

Fig 2.27 Top: when grooving try to arrange to plane with the grain. Bottom: a gauge for testing the thickness of panel edges.

As with the rabbet plane, short cuts are first made at the far end of the work, gradually increasing in length. Continuous pressure must be applied by the fence against the work. Unlike rabbet planing where no harm is done, failure here will result in a false cut being made too close to the edge, an error which cannot be rectified.

The compass or circular plane

Now made only by Record, this plane (Fig 2.28) is a very expensive tool for the amount of work it can produce. Its flexible sole adjusts to any required curve. It is excellent for long gentle curves which are difficult to achieve using a spokeshave.

Fig 2.28 The Record circular plane.

The block plane

This small, single-handed plane (Fig 2.29) varies between the very crude and the precision models. The better versions with a single cutter, set bevel up at angles of 20° and 12°, are provided with cut and

Fig 2.29 Low angle block plane with adjustable mouth.

lateral adjustment and also a sliding mouth. These are useful planes for small jobs or details, for end grain work or for cleaning up difficult grain.

Fig 2.30 "Three-in-one" planes combine the functions of the shoulder, bullnose and chisel planes.

Spokeshaves

Spokeshaves can be divided into two distinct styles. The first of these is the flat face, which is used for working convex curves, and the second is the round face, which is used for working hollows. The metal versions of the tool illustrated in Fig 2.31a and b are now the most common, popular and easily obtainable. The heavier model is provided with two thumbscrews, making precise adjustment easy while the lighter model with no adjustment and straight rather than cranked handles is, nevertheless, a very pleasant tool to handle, particularly on fine work. All are sharpened in the same manner as plane irons. The cutters, being small, require a simply-made wooden holder for use on the oilstone or grindstone (Fig 2.32).

The older wooden spokeshaves in beech or boxwood (Fig 2.33) are a pleasure to use and are still popular with many woodworkers. After a long

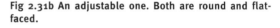

Fig 2.31a A light non-adjustable iron spokeshave.

Fig 2.31b An adjustable one. Both are round and flat-faced.

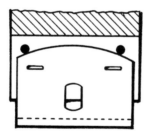

Positions and purpose of pins

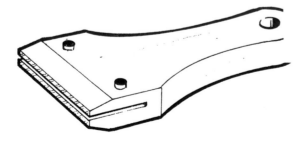

Fig 2.32 Holder for sharpening the blades from metal spokeshaves. Pins are normally tapped flush.

gap they are now on limited sale again and, of course, there are second-hand ones about. These may well need re-mouthing in either ebony, rosewood or brass. Check the blade very carefully before you buy one, however, as replacement blades are not available unfortunately, so there is very little that can be done to salvage a wooden spokeshave with a well-worn blade.

Blades for wooden spokeshaves are most conveniently held in the vise while a flat slipstone is used to sharpen them. The maker's angle should be preserved on the top, not allowing it to develop too steeply. The bottom face must stay completely flat with no trace of a bevel. Adjustment is made with light hammer taps. If the tangs have become sloppy in their holes, thin slivers of wood can be glued in, using the tapered tangs to clamp them in place. Later the holes can be pared or filed down to a good working fit.

Compared with the iron bench planes, the spokeshave is a rather poor tool, lacking the fine adjustment of mouth. Therefore it is most important that the tool is always worked *with* the grain, no matter what the shape of curve involved. Unlike planing, this involves frequent changes of direction.

Fig 2.33 Traditional wooden spokeshaves like this one are becoming available once more in limited numbers.

Any attempt to work against the grain will result in the wood tearing, no matter how gradual the shape of the curve.

The direction of cut is illustrated in Fig 2.34a and b. In Fig 2.34a the spokeshave works down into the hollow, from the left, then down again into it from the right. At the highest point the direction is changed to complete the shape, end right. In the common circular application shown in Fig 2.34b work always towards the end grain.

Watch carefully the finish being produced, since according to the run of the grain, the change of direction point may not always be where expected.

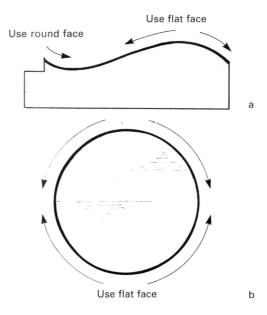

Fig 2.34 Direction of cut and face used when using a spokeshave.

Saws and Sawing

Saws can be divided conveniently into two groups – ripsaws and crosscut saws. Ripsaws are designed to cut along the grain – that is, along the length of a board. Crosscuts are for cutting across the width of the board and generally for joint cutting.

These two groups are distinguished by the shape of their teeth. Ripsaws have from 3 to 6 teeth per inch – 4½ is the most common and 6 teeth per inch is termed half rip. The number of saw teeth is always counted inclusively. The teeth are shaped and

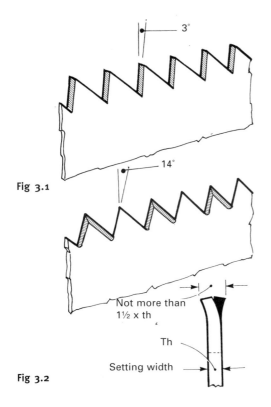

Fig 3.1

Fig 3.2

Fig 3.3 Ripsaw. Length 28 in., 4½ teeth per inch (half rip 6 teeth per inch).

Fig 3.4 Crosscut handsaw. Length about 26 in., 6–8 teeth per inch.

Fig 3.5 Panel saw. Length about 20–22 in., 10–12 teeth per inch. Note the elegant handle.

sharpened as in Fig 3.1, filed straight across to give chisel-like teeth which remove small shavings. This saw is rapidly being replaced by small circular saws or portable jig (or saber) saws. The family of ripsaws includes also the bowsaw, the keyhole saw and the coping saw. The dovetail saw (see page 33) is sharpened as a ripsaw. The teeth of crosscut saws range from 4 per inch on large saws for heavy work, to 12 teeth for panel saws and below 20 for small fine work. The teeth, shaped as in Fig 3.2, are filed across at an angle, giving knife-like points which sever the fibers without splintering. In the middle of the range, rip and crosscut merge giving dual purpose saws but, at the extremes, it is not possible to substitute ripping and panel saws.

Using Handsaws

Ripping – starting the cut

Particular care is needed when sawing components to the right size. A careless cut that results in a piece of wood being just slightly too short is an easy mistake to make and it cannot be corrected easily. The method described below should guarantee accurate results when sawing.

Begin by drawing the blade up for several strokes, guided by the left-hand thumb. Remove the left hand and commence with push strokes. Keep the saw low at first to ensure an accurate start. Once the line is established, raise the saw to a convenient angle of about 45°. Check it is vertical by using a try square. Handsaws are not often used on the bench, as it is inconveniently high. A plank should be supported on trestles or substitutes. Aim to saw just clear of the gauge or pencil line to allow subsequent planing to the finished dimension.

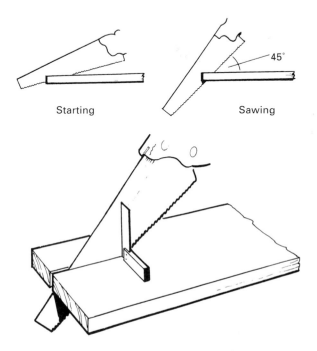

Starting

Sawing

45°

Fig 3.6 Handsawing. Keep saw vertical and check with try square.

Crosscutting

The work should be similarly supported but the cut should not be made between the trestles. As the cut nears completion, the plank sags and the saw sticks. The offcut must overhang the trestle, supported by the free hand or a helper. The subsequent start and sawing procedures are as already described.

Bench sawing, using backsaws

It is essential to hold and support the work well. For small pieces, a benchhook or sawing board (Fig 3.7) should suffice. The alternative benchhook or sawing

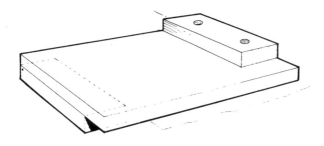

Fig 3.7 Traditional sawing board or bench hook for a right-handed worker.

Fig 3.8 Gents backsaw. They are available in lengths of 4–6 in., 20–30

board (Fig 3.9) is suitable for small pieces and use by beginners as it enables the piece of work to be clamped. Larger work needs two sawing boards to keep it level. Important cuts can be made with the work clamped to the bench with scrap wood or hardboard beneath to protect the bench top.

Start preliminary work and minor cuts by simply drawing the saw back for a few strokes, as with the handsaws. Mark important lines with the marking knife which, unlike the pencil, has no thickness. For

more precision, particularly by beginners, chisel a small notch at the far corner, in the waste, lay the saw in this and start sawing. When making important cuts, e.g., wide shoulders, deepen the knife cut strongly and chisel a shallow groove on the waste side. Lay the saw in this and draw it back a few times before sawing. A further alternative, particularly for very wide cuts, is to clamp a straightedged batten along the line and run the saw against this.

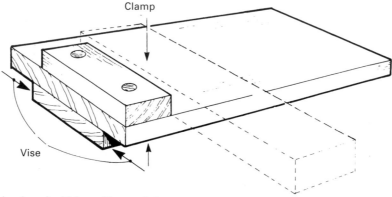

Fig 3.9 Alternative sawing board which enables work to be held firmly with a C-clamp.

The coping saw controversy

There is endless discussion as to whether the coping saw (Fig 3.10) should cut on the push or the pull. My view is it should cut on the push like its relatives, the bowsaw and the metalworker's hacksaw. In this way the line can be clearly seen, unobstructed by splintering, and the action is familiar. The exception is when the coping saw is used in the manner of the fretsaw, cutting downwards on a cutting board with its V-shaped opening. Then the teeth cut on the pull stroke, again leaving the line unobscured.

saw's hollow handle allows various lengths of the blade to be used; for example, a shorter blade for very sharp curves. The increasing popularity of the small electric jigsaw has mainly ousted these three saws.

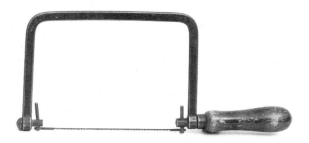

Fig 3.10 Coping saw.

Fig 3.11 Bowsaw.

Bowsaw, compass saw and keyhole saw

The bowsaw with a narrow turning blade tensioned generally by twisted cord, cuts curves in thick wood to quite a sharp radius. The bowsaw is illustrated in Fig 3.11.

The compass saw, which is sometimes part of a group of saws, is virtually a short, narrow handsaw. It is capable of cutting gentle curves, not as tight as the bowsaw, very comfortably.

The keyhole saw, which cuts even sharper curves, is particularly useful for cutting openings which the bowsaw cannot enter and which may be too sharply curved for the compass saw. It enters through a hole bored in the waste. The keyhole

Sawing tenons

The various stages in this routine task are illustrated in Fig 3.12. The procedure should be carried out using a tenon saw, an example of which is shown in Fig 3.13. As the work is along the grain and is in effect through a considerable thickness, it is certainly advisable to have a tenon saw re-cut with ripsaw teeth of about 9 or 10 per inch. This ensures a fast easy cut. The longer the saw operates in the saw cut, the greater is the danger of wandering off.

Carefully mark out the tenons using a mortise gauge and marking knife. Do not attempt to saw down more than one line at a time and do not saw down a line which is out of sight.

Start at the further corner, slowly lowering the saw until a cut of about ⅛ in. (3 mm) depth has been made right along the end grain. Tilt the component in the vise and saw to the nearside gauge mark. The saw never comes out of the initial saw cut, but do not attempt to saw to the line which is out of sight. Reverse the work or yourself and repeat the process, leaving a small triangle in the middle. Then return the job to the vertical and run the saw down the existing cuts. Saw any set-in or haunch next. Finally, saw off the shoulders, for accuracy, using the chiselled groove method described. Take care not to saw too deeply and into the tenon. If, having sawn to depth, the cheek does not fall off, then the vertical cut has stopped short. In this case, insert a chisel to

Fig 3.13. Tenon saw. They are available in lengths of 8–14 in., 13–15 teeth per inch.

snap off the cheek, then clean up. Sawing the shoulder too deeply greatly weakens the tenon. Sawing the cheeks too deep, while not reducing the strength, produces blemishes when the job is glued up.

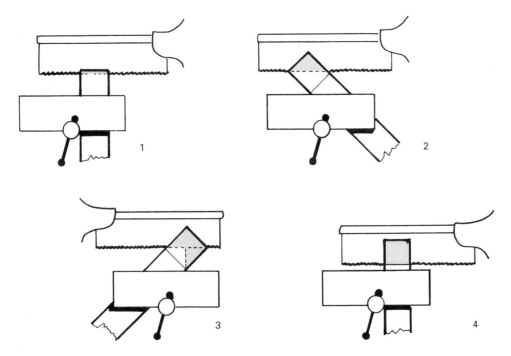

Fig 3.12 Stages in sawing tenon cheeks.

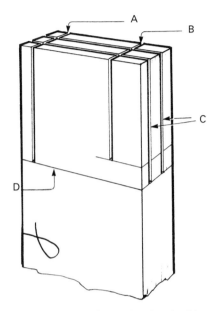

Fig 3.14 **Sawing a tenon (ready for the shoulder cuts).**

Sawing dovetails

This is precise work and great accuracy is required. This is not achieved by sawing wide and chiselling back to the mark. Both practice and confidence are needed to saw up to but not across the line. A dovetail saw (Fig 3.15) is not necessarily essential, although it is needed for small dovetails. Larger ones are quite successfully sawn with a sharp tenon saw. Once you have had to sharpen a dovetail saw, you will no doubt try to be most economical with its use thereafter!

Fig 3.15 **Dovetail saw. They are available in 8 in. lengths, 20 teeth per inch.**

The common (or through) dovetail

The tails are generally sawn first. Some woodworkers seem to find it helpful to tilt the work in order to be able to saw vertically. Having sawn the tails, the waste would formerly have been chiselled out. Nowadays, however, the bulk is sawn with the coping saw. Turning a coping saw blade at the bottom of the tenon saw cut can easily bruise the dovetail at its corner. The waste is then better removed by sawing from the middle as indicated in Fig 3.16. Remove the remaining waste by chisel, together with the sockets in the other half of the joint.

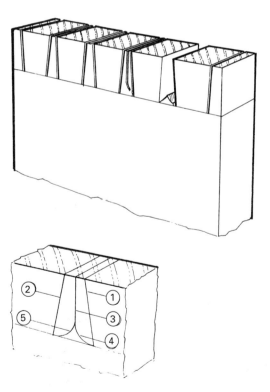

Fig 3.16 **Removal of waste from a common dovetail with a coping saw. Note stages of sawing.**

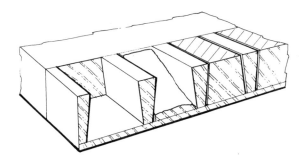

Fig 3.17 Removal of waste from a lap dovetail with a coping saw.

The drawer or lap dovetail

Cut the tails in the way just described. To form the sockets, make a diagonal cut with the tenon saw; then saw out an appreciable amount of waste with the coping saw (Fig 3.17). A chisel completes the job. The best way to clean out the corners is to have a pair of ¼ in. (6 mm) chisels, ground not square but left- and right-handed to about 12˚.

Sharpening Saws

Saws which need sharpening are the new saw that has not previously been resharpened; the well-maintained saw; the poorly sharpened saw; and the saw with broken teeth. Each needs its own special treatment, though some processes are common to all. Most steps will be covered by considering a saw which has previously been poorly sharpened.

There are two main families of saw: ripping and crosscutting. The former includes the ripsaw, the half ripsaw, dovetail saw, bowsaw, keyhole saw, coping saw and, as described later, the rip/tenon saw. The latter includes the handsaw, panel saw and tenon saw. The ripsaw family is filed across at right angles to give teeth like small chisels (Fig 3.1). You can see the cutting action by using a ⅛ in. (3 mm) chisel to simulate one tooth; along the grain a clean groove can be cut easily, while working across the grain produces a poor groove with very splintered sides.

The crosscuts are filed at an angle, giving teeth like little knives (Fig 3.2). To simulate this action, two heavy knife lines must be made across the grain and the waste chipped out with something smaller and less efficient than the ⅛ in. (3 mm) chisel.

The effect is that the ripsaw cuts easily, quickly and cleanly along the grain but makes a rough job with rather hard work across the grain. On the other hand, the crosscut cuts quickly, smoothly and easily across the grain but, while it will produce a clean cut along the grain, it makes for slower and harder work.

Saw vise

You will need a saw vise before you can start work on a saw. As this item is quite expensive to buy and will probably be used infrequently, it is worth making the model illustrated (Fig 3.18), or something like it.

The vise basically comprises two hinged jaws with spacing strips top and bottom to accept the thickness of a saw handle. The jaws can be about 10 in. (254 mm) long (or the length of the bench vise jaws) with two rounded strips on the outside to take the pressure of the bench vise. The inside capacity of the saw vise should be such that the widest handsaw will fit in. You can make a smaller vise simply for tenon saws. Line the jaws with leather or rubber to reduce the unpleasant noise of saw sharpening. One end of the saw vise jaws may need cutting away to accept the handles of small saws. An opening spring made from piano wire is convenient.

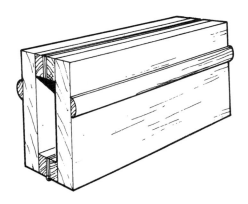

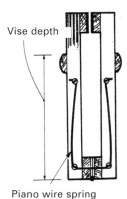

Vise depth

Piano wire spring

Fig 3.18 A homemade saw vise.

Files

First, you need a 10 in. (254 mm) second cut mill file. This should not be used for rough work; keep it carefully stored in a plastic sleeve or cloth (it can be used to sharpen scrapers and scraper plane blades).

Choose the triangle files with care as they do not last. It is important that the working face of the file should be slightly over twice the saw tooth depth (Fig 3.19); otherwise a strip down the middle of the file will receive twice as much wear as the corners. Points per inch are counted inclusively (Fig 3.20). Too large a file creates too rounded a gullet. Roll saw files in a cloth; don't leave them rattling about in a box or they may damage themselves.

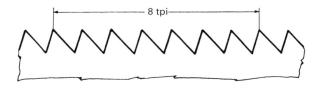

— 8 tpi —

Fig 3.20 Teeth are counted inclusively.

Choosing a triangular file

Points per inch	Suitable file
4½, 5, 6	7 in. slim taper
7, 8	6 in. slim taper
9, 10	5 in. or 5½ in. slim taper
11, 12, 13, 14, 15	4½ in. slim taper
over 16	4 in. extra slim taper
extra fine saws	needle file

Files that are 4, 5, and 6 in. are available as regular taper, slim taper and extra slim taper.

Fig 3.19 Width of file face.

If you have poor eyesight, or if you are working under poor lighting conditions, it is advisable to use engineer's blue marking fluid to show which teeth have been filed. Those old eyeglasses come in very handy for fine saws, worn on the top of the others; they magnify well but one does have to come rather close. Commercial clip-on magnifiers are also available at a price.

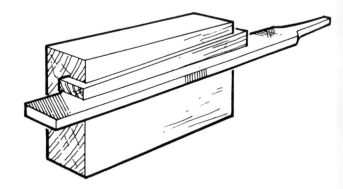

Fig 3.21 Fitting a file in a grooved block to prevent rocking.

Sharpening procedure

A saw which has been poorly sharpened in the past requires four operations:

1 Topping (sometimes called jointing)
2 Shaping
3 Setting
4 Sharpening

Topping

The teeth may be of different heights, or the edge may have been sharpened hollow (or round) or both. Fix the saw in the vise, hold a mill file (without its handle) along the blade and square to it, then run it along the length of the saw. Rocking the file, since this will round over the teeth, can be prevented by holding the file in a grooved block as illustrated in Fig 3.21; for this, the saw must be raised well above the vise jaws.

Topping produces a shiny area on the top of each tooth (Fig 3.22); make sure that each tooth has one of these (a wipe of the blue marking fluid is helpful here). If engineer's blue cannot be obtained, the shiny areas can be blacked by using a thick black felt marker instead. Formerly teeth were blacked by smoke from a candle but this particular method is not to be recommended.

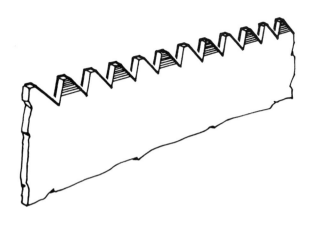

Fig 3.22 Topping teeth.

Shaping

First select an appropriate triangular file. Hold the file horizontally at right angles to the saw, and twisted to an angle of 14° to the vertical for crosscut saws and 3° for ripsaws (Fig 3.23). Some people prefer less than 14° but the angle should be substantial. These are the theoretical angles and individual saws may have been cut slightly differently; the angle can be found from the unused teeth by the handle.

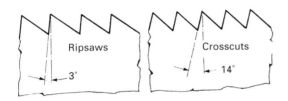

Fig 3.23 Shaping teeth.

File half of a shiny area with the file in one gullet, then the remainder with the file in the next. Once these shiny areas are filed away, top again to give each tooth a shiny area; this method prevents the spacing being lost and ensures teeth of equal height. A useful aid is a partly used saw file which has had the teeth ground off one side (Fig 3.24); this permits a bad tooth to be filed without danger to a good one.

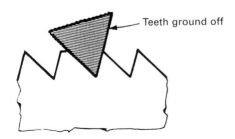

Fig 3.24 A file with one face ground is helpful.

Maintaining the angle of 3° or 14 ° is difficult; the wrist tires quickly by rigidly holding that angle and if work is interrupted it is difficult to pick up exactly the same angle again. There are helpful devices, including a commercial saw filer which appears attractive and works well, but needs special tangless files which are not commonly stocked; also the file is large, thus making work on fine tenon saws impossible. Or you can make the device shown in Fig 3.25. Turn or whittle a decent handle and fit it with a tight metal ferrule. Make a second ferrule to fit over this and rotate it. Solder a threaded nut or block to this outer ferrule and continue the thread through. A 4 in. (100 mm) rod with a screwdriver slot screws into this and clamps on the inner ferrule. To use, settle the file firmly in a good gullet, swing the rod horizontal or vertical according to preference and lock there. It will be much easier to maintain the angle using this rod as a guide or sight.

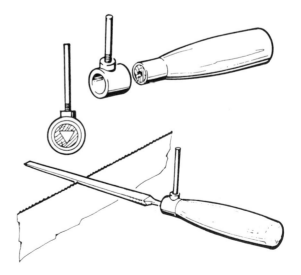

Fig 3.25 A simple angle guide.

The shaping process is complete when all the teeth have lost their shiny areas and the gullets are all the same depth.

Setting

Teeth are bent to alternate sides, so that the saw doesn't bind in the kerf. Setting should be arranged so that the kerf will be no more than 1½ times the sawblade thickness. Softwoods require greater set than hardwoods and wet wood more still. Taper-ground handsaws require very little set. It is vital that each tooth be given exactly the same set; if not, the saw will want to run out of line, a fault often incorrectly attributed to teeth not holding their edge. Only the top half of a tooth should be set. Never attempt to reset teeth to the opposite side: this will cause cracking and loss of teeth, as will trying to

bend over the whole tooth. The most common fault in home-maintained saws is oversetting.

The pliers-type saw set offers the best setting method to the amateur. Several patterns are on the market but examine them carefully before buying. One make will cope with only less than 12 teeth per inch; another can be dismantled and filed to do smaller work. The Stanley 42SS has between 4 and 16 tpi and is one of the best currently available. The Disston No. 28 has 4 to 10 tpi while the No. 280 has 10 to 16 tpi.

In the absence of a saw set, or for setting very fine teeth (see Fig 3.26), the following method is recommended. Carefully plane a short length of 2 in. (50 mm) thick hardwood on one end grain, and grip it in the vise. Secure the saw to it with two wood-screws and large washers. The set is put on alternate teeth using a fine punch, preferably brass, giving two

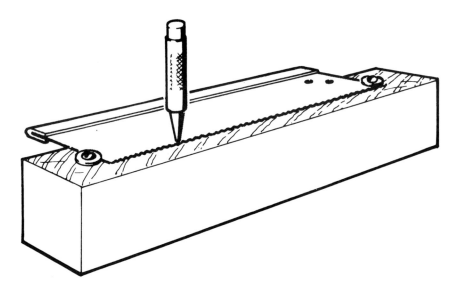

Fig 3.26 Setting very fine teeth.

or three light blows with a small hammer. The saw is turned over and the process repeated.

After setting, place the saw flat on the bench and lightly run an oilstone along the teeth; turn over and repeat. This corrects the odd tooth which may be too prominent, thus preventing a jump when sawing.

Sharpening

Different methods are used for sharpening saws that belong to the ripsaw and crosscut families. Ripsaws are sharpened at 90°, in the same manner as the teeth were reshaped. Fix the saw in the vise with the handle to the right. Top the saw again, very lightly putting a small shiny area on each tooth. Now wipe blue marking fluid on the teeth. Then file at right angles to the saw and horizontally, starting on the front edge of the first tooth set toward you and

continuing on alternative teeth (Fig 3.27). Two or three steady push strokes should be enough to take off half of the shiny area. It is the front edge of the tooth towards you that gets the filing; this puts any roughness on the tooth to the inside, where it has no effect and is lost in work. The blue marking fluid helps, particularly with small saws, to make sure that two adjacent teeth are not filed. At the end, reverse the saw, and saw vise also if preferred (handle now on the left), and continue to file the front edge of the tooth set towards you. Do not save time by filing every tooth at 90° from the same side: it makes the saw run to one side.

Crosscut saws are sharpened at an angle, not at 90°, giving bevelled teeth producing knife-like edges. A long, thin bevel on a tooth (Fig 3.28) cuts well for a time, particularly on dry hardwoods, but quickly wears, so a shorter bevel is more suitable for general use.

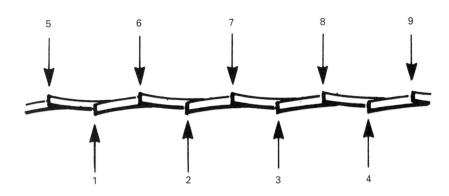

Fig 3.27 The order of strokes when sharpening a saw used for ripping.

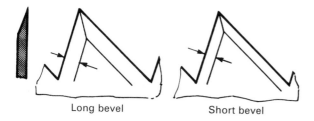

Fig 3.28 Sharpening a saw used for crosscutting.

Again, fix the saw in the vise, projecting about ¼ in. (6 mm) with the handle on the right and lightly top all the teeth. Wipe blue marking fluid on them at this stage. Begin filing on the front edge of the first tooth set towards you (Fig 3.29). Move the file handle to the left, making an angle of 65° to 75° depending on

preference and the type of lumber you expect to work: softwoods take a thinner bevel, hardwoods a thicker one. Maintain this angle, filing alternative teeth and removing half of the shiny area. It may be helpful to mark this angle in pencil on the top of the saw vise jaws. On reaching the end, reverse the saw (handle to left) and repeat, removing the remaining half of the shiny area, keeping the file horizontal at all times.

The saw is now fit for use. Having done this amount of work, it is preferable not to have to do it again too soon as a result of damaging the teeth. Therefore look after the saw carefully. Do not let it rattle around with other tools, carried in a box or bag, or let it bang about in the workbench storage area with clamps, hammers and the like. You may find silicone sprays useful in combating both friction and rust.

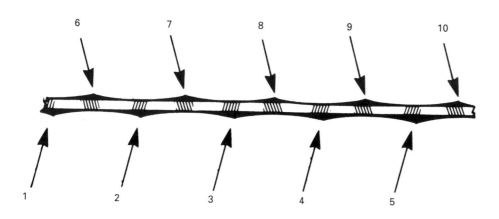

Fig 3.29 The order of strokes when sharpening a saw used for crosscutting.

Angles

Once you are experienced, angles become a matter of personal preference. The angles stated are about 14° front angle for a crosscut saw and about 3° for a rip. These are the angles which Spear & Jackson say they put on their saws; their tenon saw, being a crosscut, is given 16°. Disstons claim to put on 15° for a crosscut saw and 8° for a ripsaw. When the angle to the front of the tooth is appreciably more than recommended it is described as having too much "hook" or pitch and may jolt suddenly in the cut which could cause a kink in the blade.

Fine dovetail saws have such small teeth that, if they were filed front and back at say 70°, there would be no tooth left so it is best to sharpen them with a needle file at 90°, as for a ripsaw. As most of their work is with the grain this is no disadvantage.

Rip tenon saws

To saw through a 2½ in. (65 mm) board, one would use a ripsaw of probably 4½ tpi, the saw built for the job. For sawing the cheeks of a 2½ in. (65 mm) wide tenon, most woodworkers use a tenon saw of 15 tpi whose teeth have been specifically filed for crosscutting. This really doesn't make sense so I suggest, instead, you make a rip tenon saw.

Obtain a second tenon saw with sufficient depth of blade left to cope with the average tenon. You will also need an old power hacksaw blade of 9 or 10 tpi. With the mill file, file off the teeth from the tenon blade. Clamp the hacksaw blade and the tenon saw together in the saw vise and, using the hacksaw blade as a guide, file the new teeth until the hacksaw blade stops further filing; this is a bit rough on the file but it only happens once. Having marked the teeth well, proceed exactly as for topping and shaping; then set and sharpen. This saw will cut tenons more accurately and rapidly than the standard crosscut tenon saw, for the longer the saw runs in the kerf the easier it is to get off-line.

Fig 3.30 A piece of metal pinned in the vise jaws provides a guide for a saw set at the saw's end.

Fig 3.31 Recutting the teeth to make a rip tenon saw.

Broken teeth

When one or more teeth are completely missing quite a lengthy job is needed. Firstly, top the saw strongly, giving quite large shiny areas. Then shape, bringing the teeth to points. Give a touch to the gullets on each side of the broken tooth so that they remain the same depth as the others. Continue topping and shaping a number of times until the new teeth emerge and are the same height as the others. Then follow the standard routine.

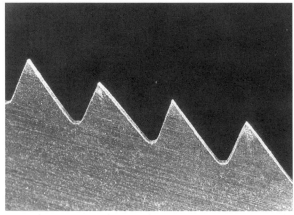

Fig 3.33 **Teeth of a well sharpened ripsaw.**

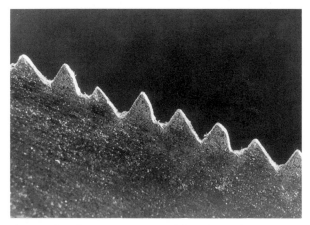

Fig 3.32 **Saw in a poor state requiring sharpening.**

New saws

Well maintained or new saws (Fig 3.33 and Fig 3.34) require the minimum of topping, just sufficient to reveal that no tooth has been damaged, perhaps by being caught on any metal. If all is well, the shaping process may be omitted for a few treatments and the sharpening proceeded with right away. Few people appreciate how little set is required, so frequently two or three light sharpenings can be carried out without resetting. A little and often can be regarded as a sound maxim for saw care.

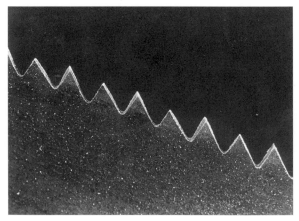

Fig 3.34 **Teeth of a well sharpened crosscut saw.**

Maintenance

A sharp saw should be well protected when it is not being used. There are several methods of making sure that the saw does not suffer any damage. You can either hang it up carefully or use a teeth guard

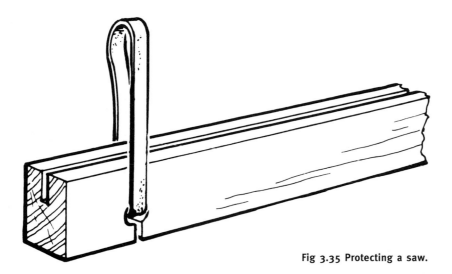

Fig 3.35 Protecting a saw.

as shown in Fig 3.35. This should be held in place with two strong rubber bands. Most damage occurs to saws when they are left lying in the storage area of the bench where they come into contact with a whole variety of other metal tools.

The blade of the saw should also be kept very lightly oiled. A carpet oil pad (a rectangle of carpet glued to a wooden block) is the most convenient way of doing this.

Sharpening requirements

The six basic requirements for sharpening saws are listed below:

1 Sharp files
2 A firm vise
3 Good lighting
4 Good eyesight (or good eyeglasses)
5 Plenty of time
6 Don't talk or, if possible, don't allow interruptions

<table>
<tr><td>

Chapter 4

</td><td>

Chisels and Gouges

</td></tr>
</table>

Chisels

Of the many varieties of chisel, five are in common use so I will concentrate on these.

The firmer chisel
This is a fairly robust chisel for bench work (Fig 4.1). Like most chisels it generally has a shouldered tang. The alternative form is the socket type in which the handle goes into the chisel.

Fig 4.2 Bevel edge firmer chisel.

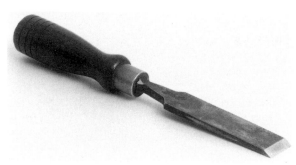

Fig 4.1 Firmer chisel.

The bevel edge chisel
This has a lighter, thinner blade, and is built mainly for paring (Fig 4.2), though it stands light taps with a mallet. It is essential for chopping dovetails, (Fig 4.3). When buying a bevel edge chisel, take care to examine the edges very carefully. Many of the modern ones are excessively thick here, which is a disadvantage when dovetailing. The old ones had beautifully thin edges.

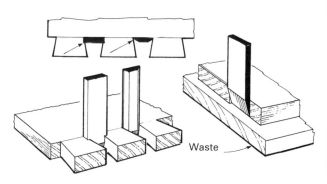

Fig 4.3 Dovetails require a bevel edge chisel. Paring into a waste block (right) prevents break-out of the far edge.

Figs 4.4 Long, thin bevel edge paring chisel.

The paring chisel

This is an extra long (often with a 10 in. [255 mm] blade), extra thin, bevel edge chisel built specifically for fine paring (Fig 4.4). It should not be struck.

The mortise chisel

As the name implies, this chisel is used specifically for chopping mortises (Fig 4.5). Its thickness is very much greater than its width (i.e. its size). The handle is massive and is generally made of beech. Its oval section is intended to give a good grip to avoid twisting in the mortise. The shoulder or flange is very large and has a leather shock-absorbing washer between it and the handle. Though much mortising is now done by machine, this is still a useful tool to have for anything other than very light work, since its great thickness enables it to stand up to the levering out of the waste, a task which accounts for many broken lighter chisels.

The sash mortise chisel

The sash mortise chisel (illustrated in Fig 4.6) is in fact a lighter version of the mortise chisel, which was originally designed for mortising sash window frames. It is sometimes referred to as the London Pattern. It has a finer handle, often boxwood, still retaining the leather washer, and it is considerably thicker than a firmer chisel of the same nominal width. The sash mortise chisel is the ideal tool for cabinet-making tasks and it is much more freely available than the true mortise chisel.

Fig 4.5 The true mortise chisel.

Fig 4.6 Sash mortise chisel, also known as the London Pattern mortise chisel.

The slick

This chisel (Fig 4.7) has little to commend it. It is a rather heavy chisel, between a mortise and a firmer chisel. A leather washer is generally fitted while the top of the handle is given an iron band. This is to prevent splitting when used, as is common, with a hammer by itinerant workmen. If a mallet is used, it is soon damaged. When chopping mortises, this tool is more likely to twist than a true mortise chisel.

Handles were formerly of the carver, bottle or octagon forms, in ash, beech or, for the better ones, boxwood. The octagon handles were invariably of boxwood. In recent years a number of different types of unbreakable plastic handle has appeared but they are not to everyone's taste, particularly when old and worn. Some manufacturers fit only one size of handle to chisels from ⅛ to 1½ in. (12 to 38 mm), arguing that the hand remains the same size whatever the chisel. This is convenient for the production engineer, but most readers will prefer a small fine handle for delicate work and a larger one for heavier work where a stronger grip is required.

Old chisels

Fig 4.7 The slick.

These are probably the most common old tools. A split handle can easily be replaced. Those blobs of hardened paint and putty can be removed. A chipped and broken edge can be ground back into use. But examine the flat face carefully. If this is pitted with rust, the tool will be of little use. With grinding and honing, some rust pits will eventually appear as small chips in the cutting edge.

Sharpening chisels

Most of the information already given on sharpening applies to chisels. The normal grinding angle should be between 20° and 25° while the honing angle should be between that and 30°. The long, thin paring chisel will have a smaller grinding angle while that of the mortise chisel will be slightly greater. On this tool, the honing angle should be kept close to the grinding angle for best results.

In direct paring, the flat side of the blade slides over the cut surface. Pare with the grain. Paring against the grain is impossible as the work splinters ahead of the cutting edge. Any trace of bevel on the flat side produces a tool which will no longer pare. As with planing, chiselling end grain causes tear-out on the far corner so this operation must be carried out on a smooth-faced block of waste wood. When making a sizeable end grain cut, the strength of the shaving will force the chisel back by a minute amount so, when cutting back to a line, make sure that the last one or two shavings are very thin and lacking this strength. In chopping back dovetails and dovetail sockets to a mark, they must all end up in

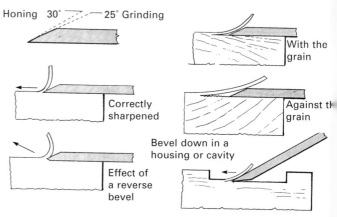

Fig 4.8

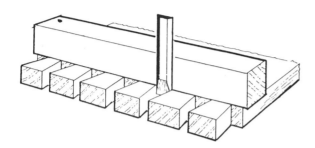

Fig 4.9 A paring block keeps the chisel vertical and the dovetail sockets in line. Sandpaper glued to the block helps.

line. To ensure this, clamp a thick guide block up to the line (Fig 4.9). This also helps to ensure a vertical cut. A strip of sandpaper cut just narrower than the block, glued beneath, prevents slipping when applying the clamps.

Do not allow the honing bevel to grow too big as this impairs performance. Generally, softer woods can take a thinner bevel than harder woods. Too thin a bevel used on end grain is liable to crumble or break. When doing a fair amount of chiselling, keep the leather strop to hand and use it frequently.

Chopping a mortise

(See Fig 4.10.) Do not mortise in the vise if avoidable. Clamp the work securely either on the bench top or, better still, to a mortising block held in the vise. If the work must be gripped in the vise, have below it a slightly thinner piece resting on the vise bars. This will prevent the work sliding downwards during the process and becoming scored.

Use a mallet, not a hammer, and pick one of a suitable size and weight. Mark the depth of the mortise with masking tape on the bevel face of the chisel only. Try to stand looking along the mortise.

Drive in the chisel near the far end of the mortise, bevel towards the middle. Check that it is vertical, using a short rule or straightedge. A long one will foul on the handle. Withdraw the chisel, then drive in again, perhaps ⅛ in. (3 mm) away, with the bevel facing the first cut. Break off the chip by pushing the handle forward towards the first cut. Lever out the waste. Repeat this until almost the end of the mortise. This, then, is the routine:

1 Drive in
2 Break off the chip
3 Lever out the waste

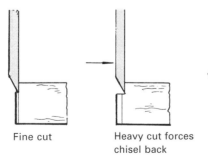

Fine cut · Heavy cut forces chisel back

Thin bevel on soft wood

Thin bevel crumbles on hard wood

Thick bevel wood crumbles

Fig 4.10

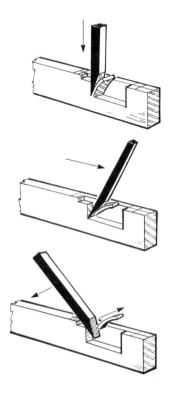

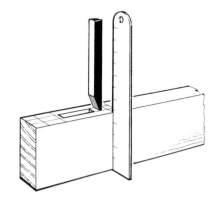

Fig 4.12 Checking that the chisel is vertical.

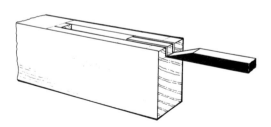

Fig 4.11 Mortising: drive in, break off, then lever out.

Fig 4.13 Making the haunch socket.

Turn the chisel round and then repeat the procedure, moving towards the other end. Carry on in this manner until the final depth is reached. Only then chop vertically for the ends of the mortise. Break off the chip, then lever out on the finger or a wood block to avoid bruising the ends of the mortise. At intervals, check that the chisel is being driven in vertically, that is, parallel to the true face.

A haunch socket is generally removed by two very careful saw cuts then chiselling, taking care to observe the direction of the grain.

The process of cutting mortises is fully illustrated in Figs. 4.11–13 and this procedure must be followed. Do not twist the chisel, do not let it move sideways and, above all, do not pare down the sides of the cavity. As the whole mortising system is geared to the width of the chisel to be used, any of these irregularities can only make the mortise oversize. Inside a mortise, accuracy is the requirement, not a fine finish.

When a pair of mortises is being cut, as for a table or stool leg, if the first mortise is chopped to

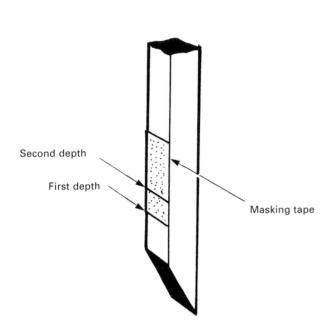

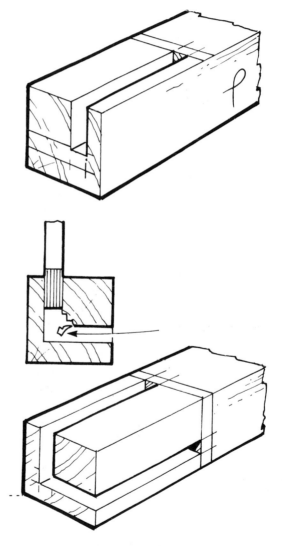

Fig 4.14 **Marking cut depth.**

its finished depth then the second will be chopped over a cavity. This frequently results in the inside corner breaking off. This can be avoided, however. Mark the first and second depth on the masking tape (Fig 4.14). The first mortise is chopped short of the finished depth. The second mortise, cut to finished depth, meets the first one without breaking out. Where necessary the internal corner can be trimmed square with a broad chisel. (See Fig 4.15)

A particularly useful addition to the range of standard chisels is a pair of dovetailing chisels (see

Fig 4.15 **Cutting a pair of mortises.**

Fig 4.16): ¼ in. (6 mm) is the most convenient size. Bevelled edges are not essential. These chisels are ground to about 10° or 12° and honed in the normal way. They are most efficient for cleaning up the corners of the sockets for lap or drawer dovetails.

The cutting of housings and halvings is clearly shown in Figs 4.17–19. When dovetailing, chop from both sides and with a small straightedge or the side of the chisel, test for flatness in the gap (Fig 4.20). A hump here will push the other component forward,

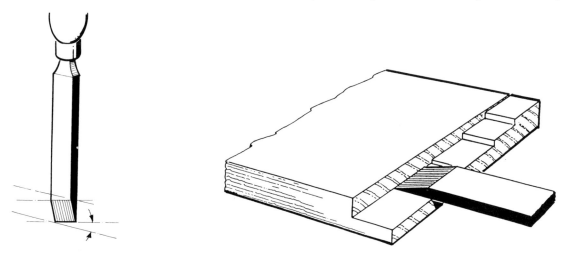

Fig 4.16 Dovetailing chisel, about ¼ in. (6 mm), with a cutting edge angled at 10–12°.

Fig 4.18 Chisel removes bulk of waste in end-grain rabbet. Watch grain direction!

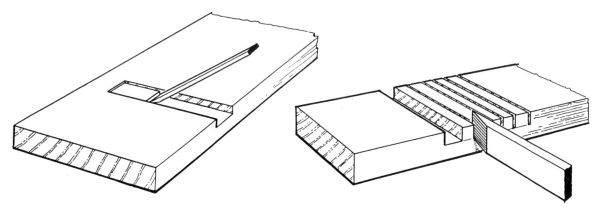

Fig 4.17 Bulk of housing waste removed by chisel, bevel down. Finish with hand router.

Fig 4.19 Removing bulk of waste in a cross-halving after weakening by saw cuts.

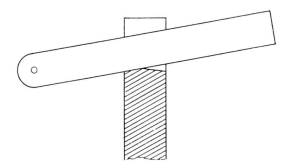

Fig 4.20 Check when chopping dovetails that the cut is flat.

out of shape. The smallest amount of hollowness will not materially affect the joint, but do not aim for such hollow sockets. If you are dovetailing in any of the softer woods you will require a longer, thinner bevel and sharper edge in order to prevent crumbling in the middle.

Gouges

For general bench work, as distinct from carving, there are basically two types of gouge. Firmer gouges are ground on the outside, and scribing gouges on the inside.

The firmer gouge

(See Fig 4.21.) This is for general bench work, for example making shallow recesses for finger grips. It is sharpened on an oilstone, like a chisel, but with a constant rolling motion. Roll sufficiently to ensure that the corners also are sharpened, not just the middle. Firmer gouges are generally ground to a slight curve. The burr on the inside is removed with a slipstone of the same or slightly smaller radius than the gouge.

The scribing gouge

(See Fig 4.22.) This can be compared to the paring chisel. In fact in its longer thinner form it is generally referred to as a paring gouge, hence it is absolutely essential that the flat sides of the tool remain so. The inside bevel is sharpened with a slipstone as close as possible to its own radius. The burr is removed on the oilstone by holding the gouge quite flat and rotating it back and forth. The difficulty of getting this gouge ground (special grinding facilities are required) means it is wise to spend that extra time honing on the grinding bevel, thus putting off regrinding as long as possible. This gouge is used mainly for scribing the sockets or cavities to match moldings, work now generally done by machine or router. It is used mostly by pattern makers.

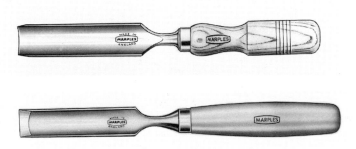

Fig 4.21 Firmer gouge, ground externally.

Fig 4.22 Scribing gouge, ground internally.

Chapter 5

Marking and Measuring Tools

The metric system is most definitely here to stay, so whatever your personal preference, you should be equipped for measuring in both imperial and metric units. As far as woodworkers are concerned, the correct metric units are the meter and the millimeter. The centimeter and the decimeter are not used.

The steel tape
The steel tape generally copes with both systems. It is pocketable and, besides being useful for initial and rough measurements, it is handy for testing squareness by measuring diagonals.

The folding rule
For a long time the most popular with woodworkers, folding rules are not often scaled in both units. The small and neat, 2 ft. four-fold has always been the preference of the cabinet maker while the larger work of the joiner and carpenter has led to them choosing the 3 ft. Metric has brought in the four-fold meter rule and a six-fold zigzag rule. This latter fits conveniently into pockets but lacks rigidity.

The rigid rule
A 3 ft. rigid rule is very useful in a workshop, hung near the bench. It is not worth spending a great deal on this item. A 2 ft. (600 mm) rigid steel rule is worth spending more on. The calibrations are precise and it serves also as a useful straightedge. The steel

12 in. (300 mm) rule is the general purpose rule while the 6 in. (150 mm) is handy in the overall pocket. These two are the most convenient to which gauges and fences are set. Spend a little extra on the stainless steel models, which stay legible for a lifetime.

The straightedge
A steel straightedge is quite an expensive item in which few woodworkers will feel the need to invest. An assortment of wooden straightedges can be built up as required (Fig 5.1). Make these from very old seasoned wood, preferably taken from old furniture. Plane true on a freshly sharpened planer. Drill a hanging hole, since storing it hung will help to prevent bowing. Test for straightness by drawing a line full length, then turning end over end and repeating. Any error will be apparent.

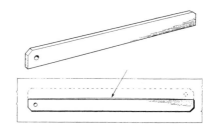

Fig 5.1 Wooden straightedge, useful in various sizes. Arrowed gap reveals error.

The try square

Next in importance to straightness comes the right angle, which is tested with the try square. Three are required, though a fourth – a smaller engineer's 2 in. (25 mm) or 3 in. (76 mm) square – is useful for dovetailing and small work. The 6 in. (150 mm) and

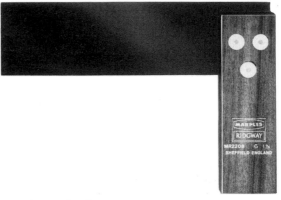

Fig 5.3 Conventional try square.

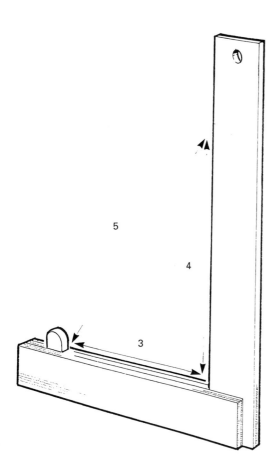

5

4

3

Fig 5.2 Large wooden try square. Make yours 3 ft. or 4 ft. Check it by applying the 3.4.5 rule of Pythagoras.

12 in. (300 mm) are the most useful sizes for bench work. My preference is for the all-metal models which generally keep their accuracy better.

For marking out large plywood and similar sheets, an all-wood model is useful. This can easily be built up from layers of ¼ in. (6 mm) plywood. Use best quality beech plywood if possible. Test by applying the 3.4.5 rule of Pythagoras.

The wood square must not be used with the marking knife. The metal squares suffer two types of damage. Frequent dropping will knock them out of square. To test this, plane or machine a straightedge and square a line with a sharp hard pencil. Turn over the square and repeat. Any error will be obvious (Fig 5.4). Refrain from filing true, since both edges of the blade will require treatment and must end up truly parallel. Instead, with a wood block, try to knock it back, then perhaps tap the rivets a bit tighter.

After considerable use with the marking knife, the outer edge of the blade becomes worn (Fig 5.5). Here the only remedy is careful filing with frequent testing.

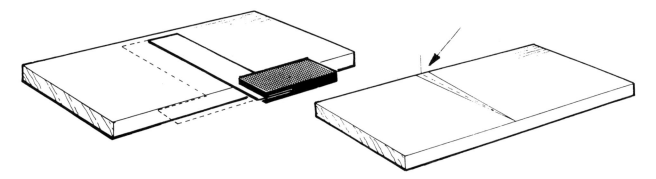

Fig 5.4 Testing a try square. The arrow indicates the error.

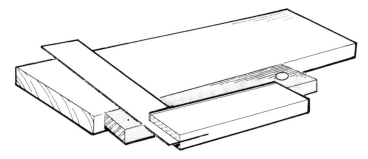

Fig 5.6 Marking an angle by means of an interposed tapered block.

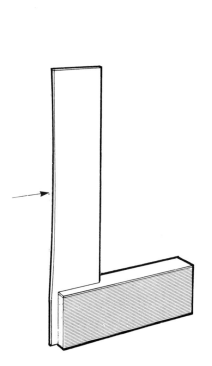

Fig 5.5 Try square showing wear after considerable use with marking knife.

Sliding bevels

These are necessary for angles other than right angles. Some are tightened with a clamping lever which is more convenient than having to fetch a screwdriver. Every care must be taken that the bevel is not knocked or dropped during the job. The bevel can often be dispensed with by using a taper block between the work and a try square. If the block is preserved, the precise angle can be re-used later in the job or for a correction.

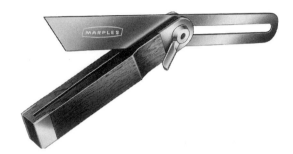

Fig 5.7 The sliding bevel.

The miter square

The miter square (Fig 5.8) becomes untrue easily. Unless you are doing a lot of mitering, it is probably not worth buying. A simplified engineer's combination square (Fig 5.9), manufactured to a lower quality, has found its way into many tool boxes and it gives a passable 45°.

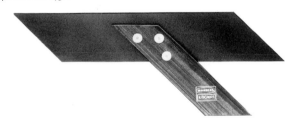

5.8 The miter square.

5.9 The combination square.

The set square

Draftsman's set squares 45° and 30°/60° in largish sizes and without thin bevelled edges are useful for checking interior angles and for accurately setting the sliding bevel. Being made of one piece they do not lose their accuracy.

Pencils and pens

Pencils are worth a mention. Apart from pencils with a medium-hard lead used for general workshop scribbling, some others are useful. A very soft pencil, which will not dent the wood, is required for marking faces and edges, identifying joints and general instructions such as top, back and inside. The traditional flat woodworker's pencil in the soft grade cannot be bettered. Many glue-ups have gone wrong as a result of confusion caused by spidery lettering with hard pencils. This tends to happen when working at speed with several helpers.

There is a lot of hostility to the use of ballpoint pen on wood. However, it has the merits of clarity and even thickness. The fine ballpoint is preferable. However, consider whether the area will later be trimmed, removing the indelible marks. If not, do not use pen.

There is no need to cut away wood to remove unwanted pencil marks. The rather coarse ink or typewriting eraser does the job well.

Early work on rough-sawn lumber can be marked out or identified by thick felt markers, hard wax marking crayons or even chalk. Masking tape can also be useful for the identification of finished or polished components where pencil marking would not be acceptable.

Gauges

Chapter 6

The marking gauge

The marking gauge is basically a marker of parallel lines which operates along the grain. If it is used across the grain, the fibers on your piece of wood will be torn. It consists of a stem, a fence, a screw and a point as you can see in Fig 6.1. In use, the fence is pushed firmly against the work, running along either the true face or the true edge. The fence is adjusted approximately and the screw is lightly tightened, then the final adjustment is made by gently tapping the appropriate end of the stem on the bench top. The screw is then fully tightened. Looking from the point end, right-handed workers will prefer the screw on the left and left-handers on the right.

When gauging a piece of work, the point should not be stabbed in vertically but should trail along the wood. The gauge runs on a corner of the stem, which is rotated in the hand to increase or

Fig 6.1 The marking gauge.

Fig 6.2 Using the marking gauge.

decrease the depth of the marking. Figs 6.2–6.4 show the process of gauging a small piece of wood held in the vise.

It is an advantage, particularly for a beginner, if the stem is drilled at a slight angle so as to facilitate this trailing action. Drill appropriately for left- or right-handed use (Fig 6.5). The point should be kept really sharp and should not project greatly: 1/16 in. (2 mm) is quite enough. Gauges are often found in school or community workshops with points which project as much as 1/4 in. (6 mm). This is actually a disadvantage and does not lead to a clean, crisp gauge line. Remember, when planing to a gauge

Fig 6.3 Gauging a small piece in the vise: the start of the stroke.

Fig 6.4 The end of the stroke. Note that the workpiece has been moved through the vise.

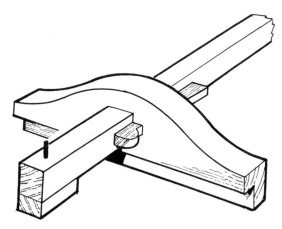

Fig 6.6 Simple panel gauge.

mark, continue until half of the V-shaped groove has been removed.

For early, rough marking-out it is convenient to use a pencil gauge, fitted with a pencil or a ballpoint or felt tip pen. This can be made especially for the job or else a suitable hole may be drilled at the other end of a marking gauge stem.

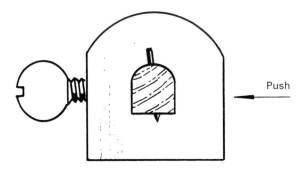

Fig 6.5 Right-handed gauge with trailing pointer.

The panel gauge

This particular type of gauge, illustrated in Fig 6.6, is no longer commercially available, so if required it is necessary to make one specially. Both the fence and the stem are much longer than the marking gauge. In the more simple version, the stem is locked with a wedge. Screw locking can easily be arranged. The panel gauge often has the pencil facility too. Because of the nature of its long and rabbeted fence it is not possible to rotate it in the manner of the marking gauge, hence extra care and knack are required for its use.

The mortise gauge

The mortise gauge, which is illustrated in Fig 6.7, works in a similar way to the marking gauge except that instead of one it has two pins for drawing two parallel lines.

As its name suggests, this type of gauge is indispensable for marking out mortise and tenon joints and it is also useful for marking out bridle joints. One of the pins is fixed while the other is moveable. The spacing between the two points is adjusted either by means of a push rod or by a screw, the latter being the preferred method.

The mortise gauge is generally made from a more exotic wood, such as rosewood. On the earlier models, the fence was locked with a slot-headed screw. More recently, a thumb screw or a knurled knob has been supplied. The spacing of the points is not set to a fixed rule but to the actual chisel, hand or machine, to be used. It should be set just a fraction below the points in order to ensure a tightly-fitting tenon.

There are often occasions, when working on a particular project, where the gauge mark or marks must be stopped short and not allowed to continue beyond a given line. Unlike pencil marks, the gauge marks cannot be rubbed out, so they are a very unwelcome sight on a polished surface, spoiling the look of an otherwise smooth piece of work. To avoid this, therefore, stab in the point or points at the finished line before gauging. Then, when gauging normally, these holes can be felt and the gauge can be stopped.

In all cases the gauges operate on the push, rather than on the pull. For real accuracy, do not neglect to use the vise, particularly if you are a beginner. You should first try to practice gauging well, then try the various fancy holdings, if you must.

The process of adjusting the width of the pins and using the mortise gauge is illustrated in Fig 6.8 on the following page.

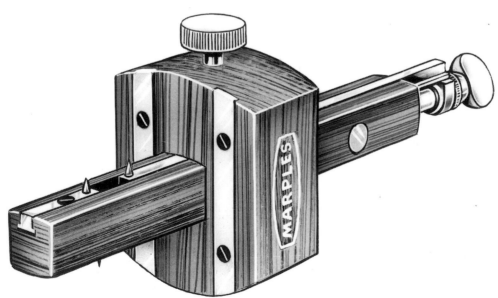

Fig 6.7 The mortise gauge.

The cutting gauge

As its name implies, the cutting gauge is fitted with a knife in place of the point. This can be seen in Fig 6.9. It has two distinct functions. The first of these is marking across the grain, where it will not splinter, as in the case of marking dovetails, while the second is the cutting of small rabbets or making a series of narrow cuts. The mark made by the knife has a vertical and a sloping side. The knife must be turned so that the vertical cut is part of the job while the sloping side is in the waste.

A bought cutting gauge can be improved by paring back the mortise at a slight angle (Fig 6.10). This has the beneficial effect of pulling the gauge into the work, which is particularly helpful in cases where the grain of the wood has the tendency to throw the gauge out of the wood.

When the cutting gauge is used purely for marking purposes, a thin pointed blade is required. For heavier work, such as when cutting rabbets, a more rounded cutter should be fitted, with its bevel toward the fence. The same cutter suits making a series of narrow cuts, but for this, the bevel faces away from the fence. Fig 6.11 illustrates the cutter shapes while Figs 6.12 and 6.13 opposite show how to cut a rabbet and a strip of wood respectively.

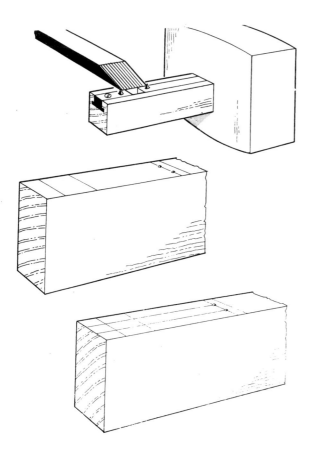

Fig 6.8 Top: mortise gauge set to width of chisel. Middle: gauge stabbed in at end of line. Bottom: gauging stops short at the stabbing.

Fig 6.9 The cutting gauge.

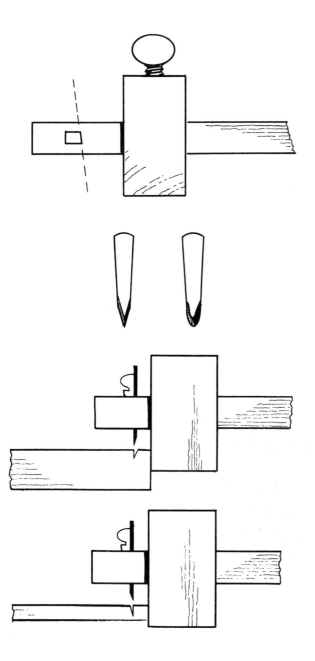

Fig 6.10 Cutting gauge mortise angled for right-hander.

Fig 6.11 Suggested cutter shapes. Left: for marking. Right: for heavy cutting.

Fig 6.12 Cutting a rabbet.

Fig 6.13 Making a narrow cut in the wood.

The marking knife

Lines to which one will later cut should be marked with a knife. The knife cut, unlike the pencil mark, has no thickness. The knife also serves to sever the fibres cleanly before sawing. A typical example would be the shoulder of a mortise and tenon joint.

There is a long tradition, from which a few tool manufacturers are now escaping, of grinding the knife with a curved bevel on both sides. It is far better that it be ground on one side only, and at a slight angle, say 30° to 40°. It can then be sharpened in the same manner as a chisel.

In use, the knife is held vertically. The vertical side of the cut must be on the job. The sloping side is in the waste. There is of course a left- and a right-handed version. If the wrong one is used, the bevel must be vertical while the knife is angled. This is sufficiently inconvenient to make it worthwhile for lefthanders to re-grind their marking knives.

Winding strips

These are essential pieces of equipment for the process of producing components to size. Their use

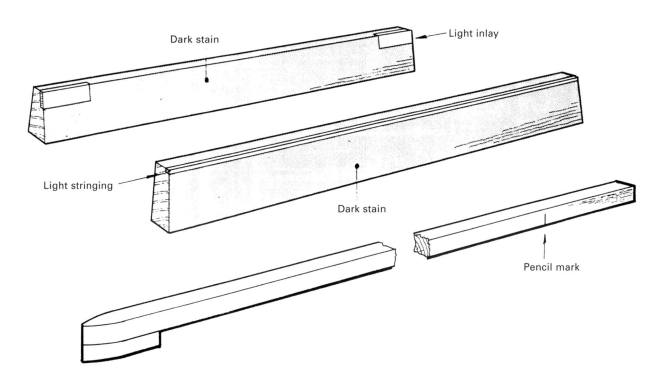

Dark stain
Light inlay
Light stringing
Dark stain
Pencil mark

Fig 6.14 At rear: winding strips with dark and light areas as an aid to sighting. Foreground: a diagonal-testing lath.

was described on page 18. Winding strips cannot be bought and therefore must be made. Many variations of a basic model can be produced according to both personal preference and available materials. One of the essential criteria, however, is that both strips should be absolutely parallel. Using dark and light woods, or masking and spraying (see Fig 6.14), will help with sighting.

A convenient-size winding strip for bench work is 1¾ x 15 in. (44 x 380 mm), while for checking larger carcasses when gluing up a winding strip about 2¼ x 32 in. (57 x 813 mm) is recommended. The strips are often tapered in thickness to improve

stability. You need to obtain some old, well-seasoned lumber, possibly reclaimed from furniture, to use for the construction of your winding strips.

Diagonal laths can be improvised but tend to be required quickly when no suitable offcuts are to hand. As they fit well into a corner, they are more accurate than a steel tape and so obviate errors of mismeasurement. The thickened end often enables the lath to span a clamp or other obstacle. Mark the diagonal lengths with a fine pencil and clean off after use. In order to keep the pointed end free from glue apply a little wax or oil with a piece of cloth before using the lath.

Chapter 7

Screwdrivers

The majority of work is still done using a traditional screwdriver on slot head screws, although cross-headed patterns and fast threads are becoming increasingly popular. The screwdrivers for this work can be divided into four groups: the conventional rigid form, the simple ratchet, the spiral "Yankee" screwdriver, and the gimmicky models which appear from time to time with great advertising, then fade away.

The slot screwdriver

The blade of this screwdriver should not be too thin, nor too stubby or rounded over. To avoid breaking, the ends of screwdrivers are not tempered to a high degree of hardness. Cheap screwdrivers, due to the use of inferior material, are not hard enough and bend in use. A good blade is sufficiently hardened that it can be reshaped with a good sharp, fine file.

The cabinetmaker's screwdriver

An old well-tried shape is the cabinetmaker's screwdriver (Fig 7.1). These are scientifically planned with the length in proportion to the width of blade so

Fig 7.1 Cabinetmaker's screwdriver.

as to apply the right amount of force to a given size of screw. Beware of the long "electrician's" screwdrivers. These are made to reach inaccessible screws. Used on small screws they easily strip the thread in the wood.

The ratchet screwdriver

Ratchet screwdrivers (Fig 7.2) are made in a more limited range of sizes. They do speed up the work but only the best have a really long life. They are particularly useful on jobs like hanging house doors where one hand is holding the work, making it difficult to change grip on a rigid screwdriver.

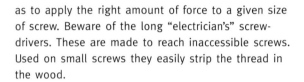

Fig 7.2 Ratchet screwdriver.

The spiral screwdriver

Developed in the United States, the spiral screwdriver (Fig 7.3) is widely copied in several sizes. Avoid extremely poor versions. For the average woodworker it is doubtful whether their high price can be justified. They do, however, offer a significant increase in torque and speed and, for the

Fig 7.3 Spiral screwdriver.

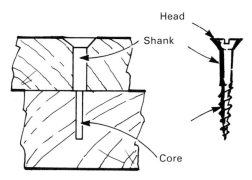

Fig 7.4

professional, the great advantage is on production work where considerable numbers of screws are being put into prepared holes. Various types of bit are available: screwdriver, drill and countersink. To avoid the spiral screwdriver bit slipping out of the screw slot and damaging the work, hold the screwhead and driver bit together between thumb and forefinger as you let the drive spring back, constantly re-centering the "push." There are also cross-head screws, of course, developed mainly for industry. The first was the Phillips head. This has now been succeeded by the Pozidriv, which has improved driving power and fast threads. The screwdrivers for each of these are slightly different.

Using Your Screwdriver

Screws should be turned in with moderate force, not driven in. In order to achieve this, when two pieces of wood are to be screwed together, the upper should be drilled to accept the shank of the screw with a frictionless fit. It may then be countersunk to leave the head minutely below the surface. The lower component is drilled to accept the core, leaving threads to bite into the sides of the hole (Fig 7.4). A touch of grease to a steel screw permits easier withdrawal at a later date. Beware of using steel screws in oak. The acid in the oak will corrode the

metal and stain the surrounding wood dark blue. Because of the high cost of brass screws, zinc-plated ones are often used as a substitute. Other finishes are black japanned, chrome and bronze plated. Where it is not feasible to countersink, for example on very thin metal, round-headed screws are used.

A range of screwdrivers is needed to fit all the sizes of screws in common use. The blade must fit the slot of the screw in thickness and in width. Too small a blade is liable to damage the screw slot, making further use difficult. Too large a blade will chew up the wood surrounding the countersinking. (See page 83 for drill sizes for woodscrews.)

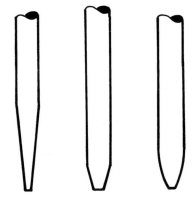

Fig 7.5 Blade taper on the left is ideal for a good quality tool. The taper on the blade in the middle is too stubby, and that on the blade on the right is even worse.

Striking Tools

Chapter 8

Hammers

The wide range of regional styles of hammer has now gone. The are two basic types left – the Warrington pattern and the claw hammer. This latter is particularly popular with carpenters and joiners. Its advantage is the claw for withdrawing nails. Today many are steel-shafted. Cabinetmakers and bench workers prefer the Warrington pattern with an ash or hickory shaft. Common sizes are an 8 oz. for general bench work and nailing, and a 3 oz. for pinning. The cross peen of the Warrington hammer is also used for rubbing in inlay stringing and crossbanding.

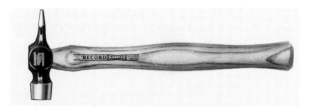

Fig 8.1 The Warrington pattern general purpose hammer.

Fig 8.2 Pin hammer, also Warrington pattern.

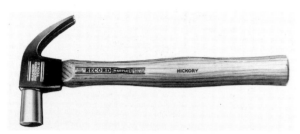

Fig 8.3 The claw hammer, more the tool of the carpenter and joiner than of the cabinetmaker.

Fig 8.4 Use of the claw hammer as a nail extractor. The wood block protects the work from bruising.

Fig 8.5 Hammer head fixing, showing metal and hardwood wedges.

Hammer heads work loose and shafts have to be replaced. There are several methods of wedging them on, that is, swelling out the top of the shaft to fit the tapered hole in the head. The method outlined below is recommended.

Make a saw cut in the shaft along the length of the hammer head. Drive on the head until there is a slight projection. Tap in a wedge of dry, hard wood. When secure, drive in a metal wedge at right angles to this. This can be bought or filed from a piece of mild steel. Finally, smooth down to the hammer head using a file and perhaps a hacksaw. Correct loose heads promptly. They are dangerous.

In addition to nailing, the hammer is used to tap joints together. Its small surface area enables the blow to be struck with precision. Work is protected from hammer marks by the use of a wood block.

Punches

Nails and pins are often concealed by punching and filling. You will require several nail punches with different sizes of end (Fig 8.7). It is worth paying a little more for a punch with a concave end as this will not slip off the nail. For marking metal for drilling, a center punch is used. This has a pointed end ground at about 60°. Punches with a square striking end will not roll off the bench.

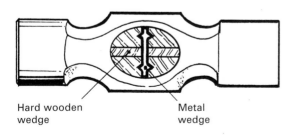

Fig 8.6 Wedging a hammer head.

Hard wooden wedge

Metal wedge

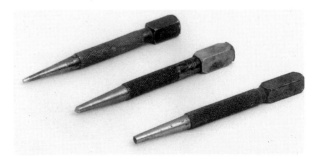

Fig 8.7 Punches. The outer ones are small and large nail punches, and between them is a center punch.

Small double-face sledgehammer

This tool was used in the past to knock together joints in post-and-beam construction. It is now primarily used for driving chisels into stone or masonry and breaking up concrete (Fig 8.8).

Pincers

Pincers may conveniently be considered here as their sole purpose is to withdraw nails. Pliers, unsuitable for this job, have no place in the woodworking kit. The jaws of pincers must close well. The better tools are ground only on the inside of the jaws, permitting them to grip even a very small protrusion. The more

Fig 8.8 Lump hammer, useful as a framing hammer.

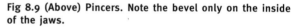

Fig 8.10 (Below) A wooden block should be used with pincers to protect work from bruising.

Fig 8.9 (Above) Pincers. Note the bevel only on the inside of the jaws.

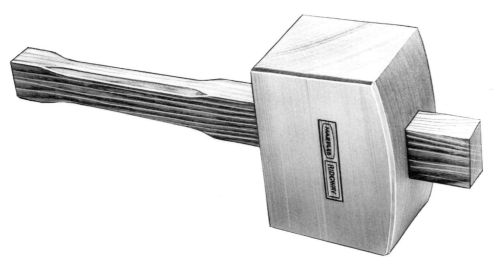

Fig 8.11 Traditional English carpenter's mallet, available in a range of sizes and weights.

common tools, ground on the outside as well, cannot grip so close. To protect the work from damage, lever on a block of scrap wood.

The mallet

The mallet has almost the sole purpose of driving chisels. It is unsuitable for assembling joints as its large surface area prohibits a precise blow. It is often thought that joints can be driven home by blows from the mallet without damage to the surface. This is untrue. Several sizes are needed, as the mallet which drives in a ¾ in. (19 mm) mortise chisel will not be suitable on a fine drawer dovetail.

For fine work on the bench, the shaft of the average mallet is inconveniently long. Readers who choose to make their own mallets would be well advised to consider a shorter handle. Many workers, especially for chopping out dovetails, prefer the

round mallets of the carver. Two shapes are made, in a variety of weights. For the gentler, close-up work these mallets have much to commend them. They can easily be turned from dense hardwood if access to a lathe is available.

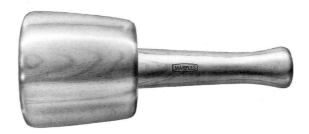

Fig 8.12 Round carver's mallet, favored by many bench workers for light work such as chopping dovetails.

Holding Tools

Clamps

The C-clamp

These clamps are universally used and differ only in manufacturers' details. Avoid the cheaper versions made in cast aluminium alloy as they break when pressure is applied. The capacities run from 2 in. to 12 in. and they are used for gluing and laminating and also for holding work firm on the bench top when working it.

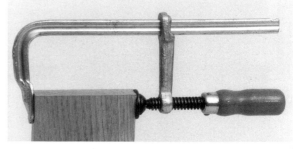

Fig 9.2 European-style adjustable clamp.

Fig 9.1 The standard C-clamp.

Adjustable clamps

An increase in use of the European form of sliding bar adjustable clamp is occurring. These clamps cover a wider range of sizes and are available in a light and a heavier form. For applying really heavy pressure the C-clamp cannot be improved upon, but the European type has a relatively deeper throat.

Lever cam clamps

For lighter work, the wood and metal lever cam clamps are useful. They are light and cheap, and are popular with model makers and musical instrument makers, whose work will not support heavy clamps.

Handscrews

The traditional handscrews are now virtually extinct but the modern fast-adjusting handscrews with metal threads (Fig 9.3) are fast gaining ground. The handscrew and the wooden lever cam clamp, unlike all others, do not require wood blocks to protect the work from damage. When working alone, the handling of work, clamps and wood blocks can be awkward.

Fig 9.3 Modern improved handscrews. They give good pressure, will grip at extreme tips, hold tapered work and require no clamping blocks.

The sash clamp

This type of clamp is indispensable for pulling together frames and carcasses of most sizes. Sash clamps vary in capacity from 18 in. to 78 in. There are two patterns with rectangular bars, ¼ x 1¼ in. and ⁵⁄₁₆ x 1½ in., and two with T section bars, ¾ x 1¾ in. and ⅞ x 2⅝ in. Extension bars are available for all (Fig 9.4). This clamp is also useful when gripped in the bench vise to hold shaped or tapered pieces for planing.

The bench holdfast

The bench holdfast is designed specifically to hold down jobs on the bench while they are in the process of being worked. Modern bench holdfasts are supplied with steel bushes which, when let into the benchtop, prevent the hole from becoming enlarged with use.

Fig 9.4 Conventional sash clamp with extension bar. Heavier model with T-section bar is available.

Light strip-metal clamps

Light strip-metal clamps (shown in Fig 9.13 on page 74) are a total waste of money, in my opinion, since pressure can quite easily bend them out of shape. It is surprising in fact that anyone buys them.

Using Your Clamps

One clamp is generally of little use. You will probably find it necessary to invest in at least two or, better still, four of the same size and pattern. Sash clamps and C-clamps tend to be most frequently used in the majority of workshops.

When gluing up a flat frame, the clamp bars must be positioned in the middle beneath the rails. If

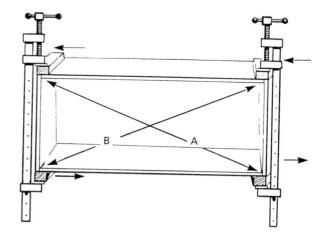

Fig 9.6 If diagonal A is long, move the clamps in the direction shown.

you find the diagonals to be unequal, i.e., A is long and B is short, move the clamps and their blocks in the direction of the longer diagonal as shown in Figs 9.5 and 9.6. Check the diagonals again to ensure that they are equal this time. A try square proves inadequate for larger carcasses (Fig 9.7) so you will need to use diagonal-testing laths as described on page 63 instead.

In the end view, the pressure is directed by the clamping blocks along the middle line of the rail (Fig 9.8). If the block is set low, as on the table shown, the component – in this case, the leg – will rotate, causing the joint to open.

A carcass is clamped front and back, though for simplicity only the front is shown here. Clamping blocks for a carcass must extend for the full width of the job, be stout enough and be slightly curved to give pressure at the middle. This is essential when gluing in a middle shelf or partition where clamps can only grip near the edge (Fig 9.10).

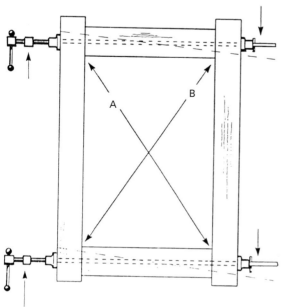

Fig 9.5 Clamps are moved in the direction of the long diagonal.

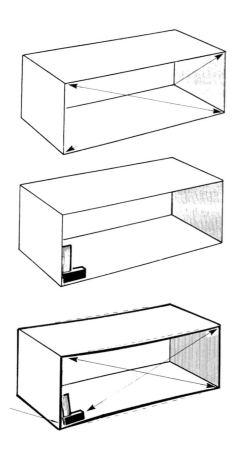

Fig 9.9 Slightly curved clamping blocks to give pressure in the middle.

Clamping blocks are an important addition to your workshop equipment. Therefore they should be made to suit, rather than just being picked out from the rubbish box.

You can prevent them from sticking to the job in hand by applying a coat of wax. If you are working single-handed, masking tape can be used to hold the blocks in position while the clamps are applied. The importance of a "dry run" cannot be overemphasized.

Fig 9.7 Top: diagonals equal, carcass square. Middle: try square is inadequate for large carcasses, especially as (bottom) over-clamping creates false reading.

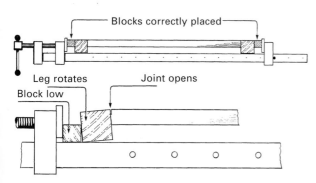

Blocks correctly placed

Leg rotates   Joint opens

Block low

Fig 9.8 Correct placing of blocks.

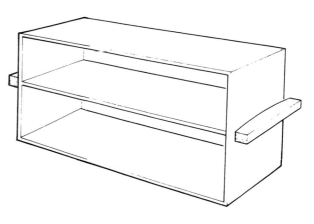

Fig 9.10 Curved blocks are essential when clamping shelves or partitions.

Fig 9.11 Holding shaped or tapered components
for planing.

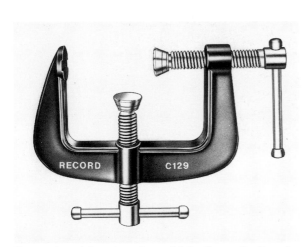

Fig 9.12 An edging clamp is useful for the application of
hardwood lippings to plywood or edges to panels faced
with plastic laminates.

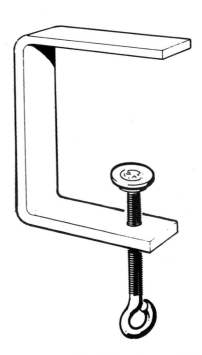

Fig 9.13 A cheap and inefficient clamp made from strip
metal usable for only the lightest of work.

Sash clamps have an irritating habit of falling over, generally halfway through a glue-up. This can easily be overcome by making several pairs of wooden feet. No sizes or shapes are important, except that the slot should be a good fit on the clamp bar.

Another clamping problem is the appearance, after a glue-up, of ink-like stains, particularly on oak. These are caused by the combined action of the water in the glue, the acid in the lumber, and the iron of the clamp bar. This, too, is easily cured. Make a few saddles from brass or aluminium offcuts. Sizes are unimportant except that the saddles should be a snug fit on the clamp bar. These will lift the work-piece just clear of the clamp bar, so preventing staining, since brass and aluminium are not affected in this way.

The Bench Vise

When purchasing your vise, there is no doubt that you should buy the very best you can afford. The 7 in. model, measured along the length of the jaw, is really the minimum for serious work. The professional may wish to go to the larger size of 9 in. or 10 ½ in. There is a choice between quick release and plain

Fig 9.15 There is a choice of flush jaw (right) or protecting jaw (left).

Fig 9.14 A popular, quick-release bench vise by Record. Jaw widths of 7, 9 and 10½ in. are available.

screw models. If funds are short, go for the largest plain screw model you can afford. There is always a dearth of second-hand vises.

The range of Record vises (see Fig 9.14) seems to be supreme at the time of writing although there are several good rivals. Beware of imitation Record vises from the Far East. As the vise is the single most expensive hand tool in the workshop, you will want to avoid buying it twice, so maintain it carefully. You should try to keep it lightly lubricated and, from time to time, clean the thread.

Wood jaws are essential; vises are given tapped holes for securing these. Check the thread. The choice in jaws is between a flush or a projecting inner jaw (Fig 9.15). Some woodworkers will prefer to preserve the smooth line of the bench edge, to

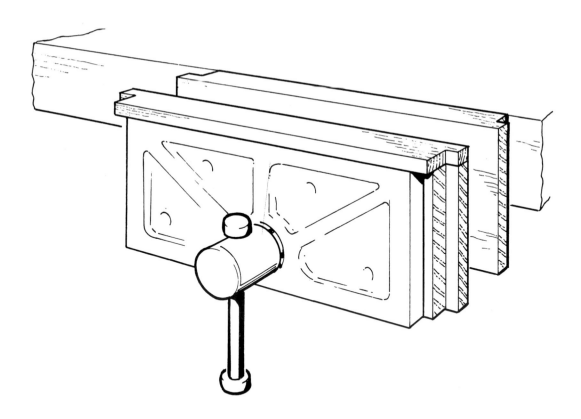

Fig 9.16 Vise jaws with modification for routing and attaching auxiliary jaws.

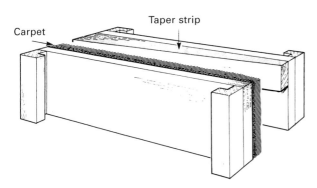

Fig 9.17 Types of auxiliary jaws for vises.

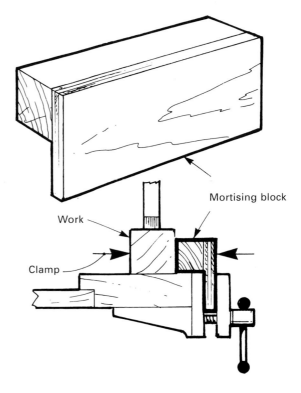

Fig 9.18 Use of a mortising block in a vise, also mentioned on page 47.

facilitate gripping long boards with the vise and an extra clamp. However, against this is the equally strong argument for the projecting jaw, namely that the jaw can more easily be replaced when worn, that a sash clamp can easily be held as shown in Fig 9.10 and that both jaws can be rabbeted at the ends to accept auxiliary jaws. Whichever of the two options you decide to choose, it is vital that you ensure that the inner faces are absolutely parallel; otherwise you are likely to encounter holding difficulties.

It is useful if a lipping is fitted to the front or moving jaw. This not only gives protection to tools from the edge of the metal jaw but is also a useful aid for power routing.

Glue on a slip, say ½ in. (12mm) thick, and plane it level with the bench top. Run the fence of the power router along the inside of the jaw, taking a cut from the outer edge of the lipping. This is now truly parallel with the inner face of the jaw. Small components can now be held in the vise for grooving etc., the router running against the lipping (Fig 9.16). Small pieces can similarly be grooved by hand using a plow plane.

Auxiliary jaws are easily made from multi-ply and they can prove extremely helpful in solving a variety of problems. Two of the most useful types (shown in Fig 9.17) are carpet-lined jaws, which can prevent damage to polished work and a jaw with an applied taper strip which can be very conveniently used for gripping matched tapered components.

Drilling and Boring

Awls

The simplest boring tools are the bradawl (Fig 10.1) sharpened on both sides using an oilstone to obtain a sharp edge, and the awl. The most useful awl is the tapered square awl, which has four cutting edges. Both are commonly used for making screw holes, a task nowadays increasingly performed with a hand drill and an assortment of wood drills. The gimlet is virtually extinct among serious woodworkers.

Fig 10.1 The bradawl.

Bits and drills

The distinction should now be explained between a bit and a drill. In very general terms, a drill is an engineer's tool designed for use on metal, while a bit, on the other hand, is made specifically for wood. Again generally, a drill has a round shank and is held in a three-jaw chuck. A bit, however, has a square shank and is held in the two-jaw chuck of a brace. Machine bits, intended for three-jaw chucks, naturally have round shanks.

All woodcutting bits have two key features in common. These are a needle point, which permits the bit to start precisely on the required spot, and a spur or nicker which severs the fibers in advance of the router or cutter, which removes the waste within the scribed circle (Fig 10.2).

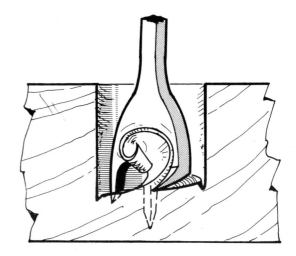

Fig 10.2 Cutting action embodying the three basic drill features.

The twist drill

This drill lacks the needle point and spur. Its stubby point makes accurate starting uncertain. Nevertheless, it is now the main implement for drilling pilot and clearance holes for woodscrews. The electric drill must now be accepted as a hand tool, doing much of the work formerly done with the hand drill.

The center bit

This is the basic form of woodboring bit, having the three features described and nothing else (Fig 10.3). Its purpose is boring shallow holes or through holes in thin wood. To avoid bursting out, commence

Fig 10.4 Support the bit on a wood block when sharpening the cutter edge.

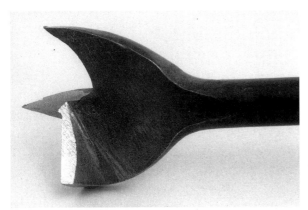

Fig 10.3 Conventional center bit.

boring from the second side as soon as the point is visible. Sadly, this excellent bit is disappearing from the catalogues.

Sharpen your bit with a fine file, filing the spur only on the inside to avoid reducing the diameter. A router should be filed on the top side only, in order

to maintain the maker's angle. Only very occasionally will the point need attention.

The successor, the fast-cutting center bit (Fig 10.5), has a screw nose to pull in the bit without the need for applying heavy pressure. Coarse and fine threads were manufactured for use on softwoods and hardwoods respectively but one is seldom given the choice. In hardwoods the larger sizes are heavy work since they pull in rather quickly. The spur and router are sharpened similarly. If a center bit is used for deep holes, it will wander off-line.

Fig 10.5 Modern fast-cutting center bit. It is available in widths of ¼–2¾ in. (6–70 mm) and lengths of 4–6 in. (102–152 mm).

Twist bits

For deep holes, several patterns of twist or auger bits were developed (Fig 10.6). They have the screw nose with a fine point, one or two spurs and one or two routers. The twist serves two purposes: It acts as a guide, preventing the bit from wandering off-line, and also as an inclined plane up which the waste is discharged. A shorter version is the dowel bit.

Fig 10.8 Traditional snail head countersink for wood.

The Forstner bit

The Forstner bit (Fig 10.9) runs virtually without a center, on its circumference. It is largely intended for shallow holes but will also cut part holes near an edge. Sharpening on the inside edge of the circumference is tedious, hence woodworkers tend to use this bit sparingly. For machine and electric drill work this has been replaced by the sawtooth machine bit (Fig 10.10). Both are quite expensive.

Fig 10.6 Solid center auger bit, commonly termed twist bit. It is available in widths ¼–1½ in. (6–38 mm) and lengths 8–10 in. (203–254 mm).

Fig 10.7 Rose head countersink bit, which has a round shank for hand and electric drills. Countersink bits with a square shank are also made.

The countersink bit

This bit is available in two forms. The more common rose head type (Fig 10.7) is primarily intended for use on metal. For the woodworker this means such tasks as deepening the countersinking in hinges and fittings. The round shank models are made for use in the hand or electric drill.

The true countersink for wood is the snail head (Fig 10.8). Its single (or occasionally double) cutter is kept sharp or extremely sharp with a fine round file, working as always on the inside.

Fig 10.9 The small Forstner bit is now becoming obsolete.

Fig 10.10 Sawtooth machine bit, now largely replacing the Forstner bit.

High-speed bits

Two types of bit have been developed for high-speed work in electric drills. The flat bit, for which three different sizes are shown in Fig 10.11, is in fact more of a scraper than a cutter, hence it will not perform at low speeds, for example in a brace. It has rather a large point, which can sometimes be inconvenient, and a scraper rather than a router. The sharp corners of this act as spurs. Sharpening is done in a small metalwork vise with a fine file, thus preserving the maker's angle.

The wood drill or lip-and-spur drill (see Fig 10.12, page 82) looks superficially like the metal twist drill. Closer observation, however, reveals that it has been ground to produce a sharp point and two spurs. The waste is removed by an action midway between cutting and scraping. These drills are tricky to sharpen but, being generally quite hard, they keep their edges well. They are available mainly in metric, down to quite small sizes. The larger sizes have their round shanks reduced to ¼ in. (6 mm) diameter.

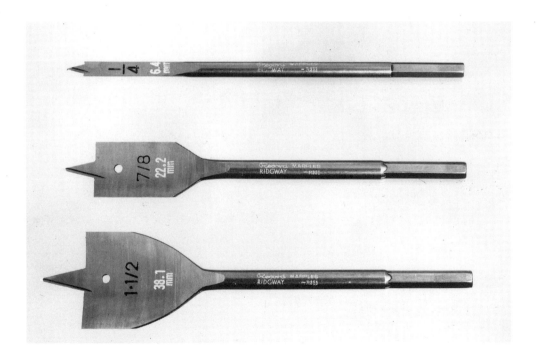

Fig 10.11 The flat bit is designed for use in electric drills. Sizes shown are ¼, ⅞, and 1½ in. (6–38 mm).

Fig 10.12 Left: lip-and-spur wood drill. Right: dowel bit.

The expansive bit

For really large, but not deep holes, the expansive bit illustrated in Fig 10.13 is manufactured. It is generally supplied with two sizes of cutter. The expansive bit will cope with holes up to a diameter of 4 in. (102 mm) or even 6 in. (152 mm), or so the makers claim. When using it to bore holes in hardwood, you will probably find that it is extremely hard work, although the process can be made a little easier if the ratchet of the brace is set to use only the pulling part of the swing.

The expansive bit is quite an expensive tool and much of its work can now be done better and more easily by a small power router.

Fig 10.13 The expansive bit for large, shallow holes.

Other drilling tools

The brace illustrated in Fig 10.14 is simple to use. The handle is rotated in a clockwise direction while pressure is exerted on the round handle at the end of the tool. Braces are available in a range of sizes. Both the brace and the hand drill shown in Fig 10.15 are too familiar and too simple to require any further descriptions. They are very rapidly giving way to power and cordless drills, which are readily available

Fig 10.14 Carpenter's brace.

from most tool shops and do-it-yourself centers and which can now be purchased relatively inexpensively. For the itinerant craftsman possibly cut off from a power source, however, the brace and the hand drill still remain indispensable.

In addition to the commonly used bits for the hand drill and brace described above, there is a whole range of bits which, although still featured in some textbooks has become virtually obsolete.

Fig 10.15 A quality hand drill with engineering-type chuck and key.

Drilling sizes for woodscrews

Screw	Clearance Hole		Pilot Hole	
Gauge	in.	mm	in.	mm
2	3/32	2.5	1/16	1.5
4	7/64	3	5/64	2
6	9/64	3.5	5/64	2
8	11/64	4.5	3/32	2.5
10	13/64	5	1/8	3
12	15/64	6	1/8	3

Chapter 11

Scraping, Scratching and Abrasive Tools

Wood can be removed in either of two ways – by cutting or by scraping. Fig 11.1 shows the cleaving action of an axe. You will see that the cutting edge, for the most part, is clear of the wood. The action of the chisel and the plane is somewhat similar; the wood spills ahead of the cutting edge, with the result that the edge is fairly long-lasting. But in the scraping action (Fig 11.2) the edge is in constant and heavy contact with the wood, so it blunts very quickly.

In addition, cutting requires less effort than scraping, and sharpening takes less time. So it is obvious that cutting is preferable/whenever possible. Scraping should generally be considered as a last resort or a special case – but it does have one great advantage: it never tears the grain.

When opting for scraping, take care that the tool works at its maximum efficiency. In actual fact, "scraping" is an unfortunate word, because it leads people to accept a very low standard of performance.

The cabinet scraper

This is basically a rectangular piece of tempered steel varying between 3 x 1½ in. (75 x 38 mm) and 6 x 2¾ in. (152 x 70 mm) but 5 x 2½ in. (127 x 64 mm) is perhaps the most convenient size. Very flexible scrapers are easy to use but they do get hot. A thick, rigid one stays cooler but tires the fingers. Having some special equipment for sharpening ensures that the job is well done rather than a hasty touch-up.

Fig 11.3 shows a set of vise jaws which not only makes the filing easier, but also reduces the amount of unpleasant noise which can result. Arrange things so that when the leather linings are in place, the jaws are naturally open just a little more than the scraper's thickness.

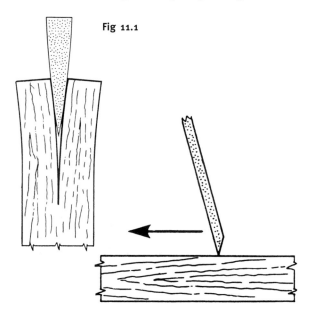

Fig 11.1

Fig 11.2

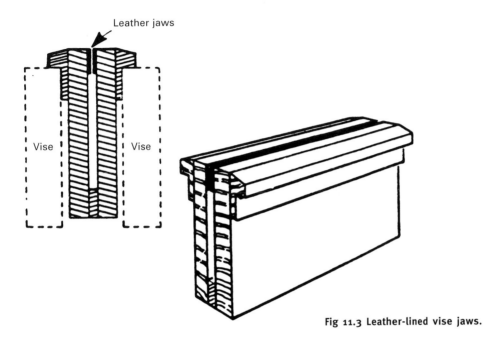

Leather jaws

Vise   Vise

Fig 11.3 Leather-lined vise jaws.

Do not stint on the file. Buy a 10 in. (254 mm) or, better still, a 12 in. (305 mm) single cut mill file. Make a fine polished handle for the file, keep it in a plastic sleeve and use it only for sharpening scrapers. An oilstone is the next tool required. Any fine (not superfine) artificial stone will serve. Lastly, you need a burnisher (Fig 11.4). All sorts of things can used for this, from the backs of gouges to ground-off files, but, if the material is not hard enough, grooves will eventually be formed in it, making the finest edge unattainable. Ideally, obtain an engineer's round lathe tool bit, 4 in. (102 mm) long by ¼ in. (6 mm) or 5/16 in. (8 mm) diameter, in high-speed steel. The cost is not excessive given that the tool lasts a lifetime. Once again, make a polished handle for it, and wrap it in a rag or plastic sleeve.

Sharpening the cabinet scraper is a procedure often described, but there are several points worth noting in particular.

Fig 11.4 High speed steel burnisher.

1 Stone the four edges flat, removing any burr from former sharpenings (Fig 11.5).
2 Set up the scraper jaws in the bench vise and file straight and square, removing all traces of former edges (Fig 11.6).
3 Finish by draw-filing, still keeping the file square to the scraper (Fig 11.7).
4 Repeat this with the stone to remove any file marks (Fig 11.8).
5 Repeat these procedures on the other long edge.
6 Remove any burr (Fig 11.5). There are now two long edges trued to 90° in section (Fig 11.9).

7 Lightly oil the burnisher and burnish the faces flat (Fig 11.10).
8 Return to the special jaws and burnish the edge with a few firm strokes at exactly 90°. This will produce edges in section as in Fig 11.11.
9 Repeat at an angle of about 85°, producing the cutting edge in section as in Fig 11.12.

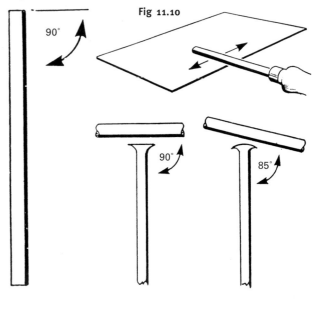

Fig 11.10

Fig 11.9   Fig 11.11   Fig 11.12

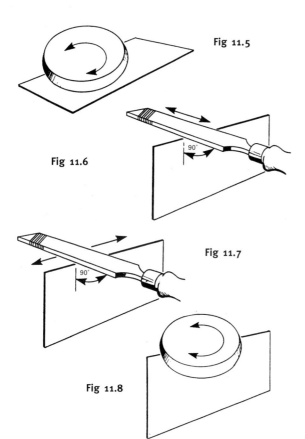

Fig 11.5

Fig 11.6

Fig 11.7

Fig 11.8

Fig 11.13a shows the cutting position when sharpened as described. In Fig 11.13b too much angle has been given in the burnishing, with the result that the tool cuts only when held at an inconveniently low angle. In use, cut not as Fig 11.14a or Fig 11.14b but as 11.14c, with a slicing action.

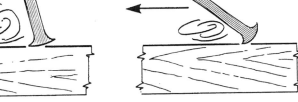
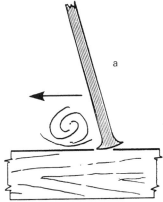

Fig 11.13

To obtain shavings of a manageable width, bend the tool by thumb pressure. Some workers tape up their thumbs with surgical tape as protection when the scraper becomes hot. Note that the scraper should be taking off shavings – thin and curling. If only dust is made, it needs re-sharpening. But beware! A flat planed surface can easily be upset by excessive use of the scraper; there is a tendency to cut away the softer parts, leaving the harder parts high. This effect becomes very obvious once the wood is polished.

Remember, too, that even the finest sanding leaves deposits of the abrasive in the pores of the wood. To subsequently return to the scraper means that its sharp edge is promptly ground off by these particles. (The same of course applies to any other cutting edge.)

As for re-sharpening, many woodworkers claim that this process can be done quickly by removing the burr, either by stoning or by burnishing, and then by burnishing the edge in the normal way. Each time, of course, the burnishing angle must be increased – until the angle of working (Fig 11.13b) becomes inconvenient. On balance, the few moments saved by avoiding making a brand-new cutting edge are not worthwhile. If the file, stone and burnisher are stored readily to hand, most readers will prefer to do the job properly each time.

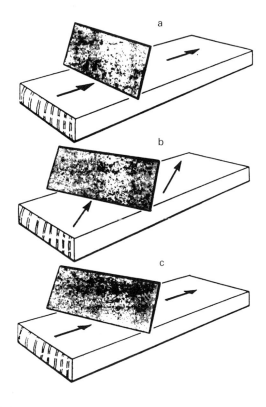

Fig 11.14

Fig 11.15 The cabinet scraper in use.

After a long interval, shaped scrapers are again becoming available, but it is always possible to file or grind a small scraper to any convenient curve. These curved scrapers are also useful for faceplate work on the lathe; for example, when removing any circular marks from the inside of a bowl. The work must be stationary, preferably with the faceplate held in the bench vise.

The scraper, though generally used to remove blemishes after planing, has other uses. It can follow the spokeshave on narrow edges. When working on the end grain of widish boards, take care that the scraping angle is different from the angle of the annual rings in the wood. Failure to do so produces a very rippled surface. The scraper can also be used to remove damaged finishes prior to repolishing.

Fig 11.16 The scraper plane.

The scraper plane

Over the years numerous attempts have been made to ease the strain which can be caused to the fingers when using a cabinet scraper, by fitting the scraper into some form of plane body (Fig 11.16). The most effective model, which is also the most common and simplest to use, is the scraper plane manufactured by Stanley. At a glance this looks rather like a giant spokeshave. There the similarity ends, however. The flat sole ensures that the surface remains true, but the length is short enough to permit local cleaning-up. The cut is adjustable by bending the blade with a thumbscrew.

The scraper plane blade is sharpened differently from the cabinet scraper. The filing angle is not 90° but 45°, which necessitates a different holding device. The one illustrated in Fig 11.17 makes it easy to file at 45° by keeping the file horizontal. Make a pair of jaws, leaving enough space between the leather strips to give an easy fit to the blade. The jaws are closed by a bolt and wing-nut. One jaw only should be glued and screwed to a horizontal strip; the other is free to move. When the jaws are dropped into the bench vise, the blade is held firmly at 45°.

To sharpen, first use a stone to remove any old edge as in Fig 11.5. Now file the bevel as in Fig 11.18. Use a stone to remove the filing burr, the file marks, and again remove any burr – in other words, sharpen like a plane iron, but at 45°. Repeat on the opposite edge. Now remove the blade from the jaws and lay it flat on the bench. Burnish the flat side as in Fig 11.10. Keep the burnisher absolutely flat (and of course lightly oiled). Next, hold the blade upright in the bench vise and burnish as follows (Fig 11.19).

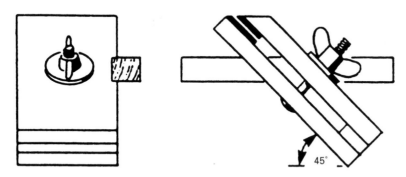

Fig 11.17

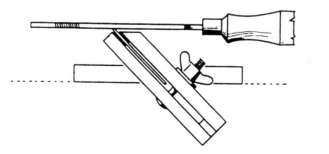

Fig 11.18

Fig 11.19

1 Lay the blade on the burnisher at just over 45°
 and give a firm stroke (Fig 11.19a).
2 Lift the burnisher to about 60° and give a firm but
 heavier stroke (Fig 11.19b).
3 Finally, holding the burnisher at 80°, give one
 firmer and heavier stroke (Fig 11.19c). The edge is
 now sharp and fit for use.
4 Repeat on the other edge.

Very carefully insert the blade into the stock,
making sure that the three screws are slack and that
the cutting edges are kept clear of metal. The flat
side of the blade leans forward; the bevel is towards
the adjusting screw. Stand the plane on a flat piece
of wood and press the blade firmly down. Hold it
there by tightening the two clamping screws. In this
position the tool may cut finely or not at all. The cut

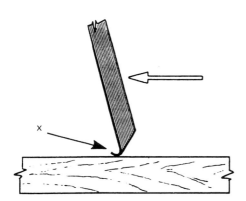

Fig 11.20

is obtained or increased by the use of the center screw. The more this is turned, the more the blade is bent and the thicker (but narrower) the shaving. Use the scraper plane in the same manner as the hand scraper – that is, parallel with the grain but with a skew or slicing cut (Fig 11.14c).

When the scraper plane refuses to cut, the cause is generally as you can see illustrated in Fig 11.20; the burnisher has been applied at too square an angle, with the result that (as shown at X) the actual cutting edge is not in contact with the wood. Bear in mind that the spare edge can be harmful to the unwary, particularly in school and evening-class workshops, so it is extremely advisable to cover the edge with surgical or carpet tape. Better still for the purposes of protection would be a short piece of the plastic spline sold for the holding of a sheaf of papers. The same material was suggested as a guard for saw teeth (see Fig 3.35, page 43). The scraper plane, too, must be held diagonally and worked along the grain. Friction is reduced by the use of an oilpad (as described on page 15) or, a more modern method, by a touch of silicone spray.

The scratch tool

From the Middle Ages until comparatively recent times the scratch tool (often called a scratch stock) was the main means of producing moldings. It is a shop-made tool, which is most useful for forming small moldings, beadings, rabbets and grooves. The scratch tool is particularly suited to cutting grooves

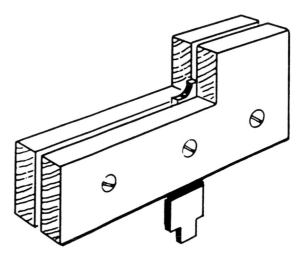

Fig 11.21a The scratch tool.

for inlaying. For many woodworkers, however, the tendency is to use the router, which with its large range of edge-forming cutters can perform the same tasks as the scratch tool.

A scratch tool can be made easily by cutting the reverse shape of the required molding in the edge of a piece of flat tool steel. This can then be secured between two pieces of wood. More detailed instructions are given on pages 92-3.

In essence then, the scratch stock is a small scraper plane with a shaped cutter. Until the final cuts, it works best with the cutter leaning forward slightly, so the sole should be slightly rounded. Fig 11.21a shows the commonly accepted form of scratch stock – but a tool like that in Fig 11.21b is much more convenient to set and use. It is much easier to adjust the sliding fence slightly than to slacken the screws and adjust the cutter. See Fig 11.22.

Ideally, cutters are made from 1/16 x 5/8 in. (1.5 x 16 mm) ground flat tool steel. This is readily available from good tool merchants in convenient short lengths. There are several possible alternatives: pieces sawn from hand scrapers or old handsaws, power hacksaw blades (carbon steel, not high-speed steel) and pieces of large band saws for instance. The material should not be too thin. Carefully file the negative of the shape required; generally, a shape is

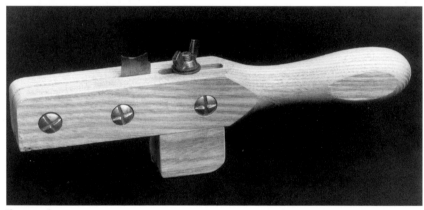

Fig 11.21b

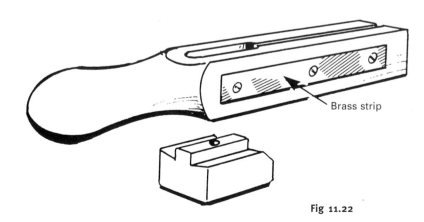

Brass strip

Fig 11.22

formed on each end. Some woodworkers file dead square, others at a slight angle of, say, 10–15°. The angle generally gives a better cut, while the square edge will cut both backwards and forwards. After filing, stone the faces flat.

If it is necessary to harden the cutter, heat it to bright red and then quench it in water or, better still, in oil. It will now be much too hard for re-sharpening. To temper it, brighten one face with emery cloth, place it on a larger piece of metal and gently warm it with a gas torch until the colors begin to appear. When light brown is reached, quench rapidly. The cutter will now keep a good edge, but it can still be filed.

Abrading tools

In shaped places where the spokeshave cannot reach, the woodworker is forced to use files. The rasp (Fig 11.23) is used for rapid removal of wood. Half round is the most convenient for general use and is easily obtainable. Round is also manufactured. The coarsest type is termed the "wood rasp" while

a finer model is known as the "cabinet rasp." Nowadays only a limited range of sizes of this tool is manufactured.

For finer work there is the wood file, which is also available in half round and round form. The coarsest is termed "bastard" and a finer version is known as "second cut." In the event of wood files not being obtainable, metalwork files of the same grades can be used, but they must be relatively new. Files of the finer grades tend to clog and so are unsuitable for woodwork. Wood files should be kept clean by the use of a steel wire brush, particularly when resinous wood is being worked.

There is continuous development of throwaway abrading tools. These tend to be aimed at the do-it-yourself market and to date do not seem to have become popular with the more expert craftsman, one reason being that they do not perform particularly well on end grain. For serious work they are no substitute for the plane (although their makers claim otherwise).

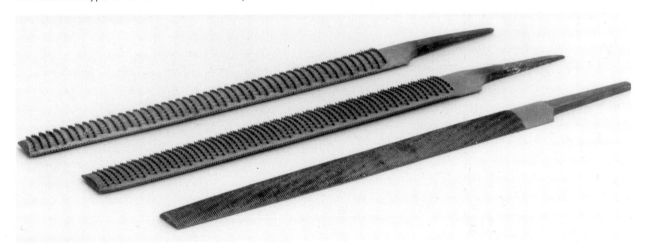

Fig 11.23 Top to bottom: wood rasp, cabinet rasp and wood file.

Abrasive papers

A piece of abrasive paper consists of many many thousands of minute scrapers which become blunt like any other type of scraper. It is the last tool to be applied to the work before polishing. Although the words sanding and sander are in common use, sandpaper as such has long since been extinct. The abrasive papers most commonly used by the woodworker are the following:

Sandpaper

Sandpaper consists literally of glass crystals glued to strong brown paper. The grades are traditionally known as super fine, extra fine, very fine, fine, medium, coarse, and very coarse. Sandpaper blunts quickly and is not now much used by woodworkers except for the fine grade, used during the polishing process.

Flint paper

Made from a natural material, flint paper was not much better than sandpaper and is now largely superseded by improved papers. The grades are termed 4/0, 3/0, 2/0, 0, ½, 1, 1½, 2, 2½ and 3.

Garnet paper

Consisting of crushed garnet, this is one of the most successful of the modern abrasive papers. It is an economical type of paper, most preferred by cabinet makers since it gives a good finish and also has a reasonably long life. It is produced as "close-coat" for hand sanding and "open-coat" for power sanding. Open coat is popular for woodturning and performs best on resinous material. Garnet paper is graded in the much more intelligible grit sizes, i.e. the mesh size per square inch. 180 is quite fine, comparable to fine sandpaper, while 60 is coarse enough for most hand work and power sanders and 240 may be used for cutting back polishes.

Aluminous oxide

This is a harder and more durable cutting material, suitable for both wood and metal. In practice it tends to be used mainly for machine sanding. It too is graded in grit sizes.

Silicon carbide paper

This paper is commonly known as "wet or dry." It is the hardest grit and provides the most expensive papers. This is little used for working on wood but the finer grades, used wet with water or white spirit, are excellent for cutting back between coats during the polishing process. Only the finer grades are used for this purpose, say 400 or 800. These papers are graded up to 1200.

Sanding

Sanding is a process which should be undertaken as seriously as planing. Well-used, blunt paper should be discarded. Halve the standard sheet lengthwise and then divide each half into three pieces. Lay the sheet on a flat surface, abrasive side down, then cut by scoring heavily along a straightedge with a scriber or compass point. This gives six pieces which fit commercial sanding blocks perfectly with no waste. These blocks are made of cork and measure

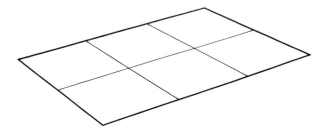

Fig 11.24 Cut or tear a sheet of sandpaper into six to fit commercial cork blocks.

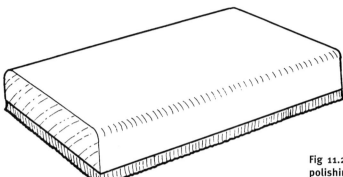

Fig 11.25 A carpet-faced block is useful in the polishing process.

approximately 1 x 2½ x 4 in. (25 x 64 x 100 mm). You can make your own blocks by gluing up layers of cork flooring tiles or by gluing one tile on to a wood block. Wood-only blocks tend to wear the paper through quickly, especially at the corners. For cutting back in the polishing process, a useful block is made from wood faced with thick carpet.

Special care must be paid when sanding edges and corners lest they become rounded over. Aggressively sharp corners, however, should be slightly softened. Test by rubbing along the corners, not the thumb or fingertips, but preferably the clenched knuckles. Sanding must always follow the grain to avoid causing scratches. However, grits of 240 and finer can safely be used in any direction. This is a clear advantage when dealing with miters,

veneers, inlays, marquetry or very difficult woods. After sanding, do not reintroduce cutting tools. The grain has become filled with minute abrasive crystals which will rapidly destroy the keen edge of the tool. Use a hand brush constantly during your sanding operations and especially when working irritant woods, always wear a dust mask. Any woodworker with allergic symptoms is strongly advised to wear one for all sanding operations.

A very useful job in the closing minutes of the working day is to glue slips of abrasive paper to small wood offcuts and dowels to make in effect sandpaper files which often prove handy for getting into awkward places. Some papers can be glued back-to-back, therefore providing stiff slips, often useful in turning and cleaning up moldings.

Mortise and Tenon Joints

Chapter 12

The flat frame

Center jointing

The simplest form of this occurs when a rail joins a stile in a center position, i.e., not at an end. This component is called a muntin. The thickness of the tenon is about one-third of the complete thickness. The mortise gauge is set not to the chosen size, but to the mortise chisel nearest to that. Gauging on both tenon and mortise must be done from the true faces. Shade in the waste. This is very important for the beginner and in cases where there is a considerable time lapse between marking out and cutting. The small "set-in" shown has no constructional value; it is cosmetic, concealing any bruising to the corner of the mortise by levering out waste, as in Fig 12.2.

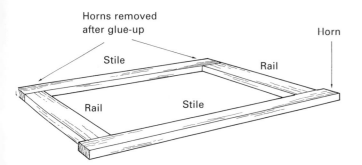

Fig 12.1 The basic flat frame.

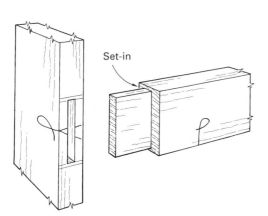

Fig 12.2a Simple joint of a muntin into a stile.

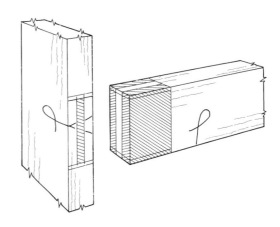

Fig 12.2b Marking out for a simple tenon.

Corners

In this case there are two additions to the joint (Fig 12.3). The set-in remains, but to avoid splitting when mortising, the stiles are left extra long, leaving a "horn." This also protects the corner during handling. In order that the mortise does not come right

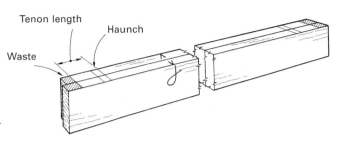

Fig 12.4b Rail marking.

The rails are gauged first, then offered up to the stiles for the markings to be transferred (Fig 12.5).

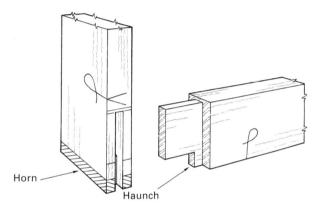

Fig 12.3 Joint at frame corner.

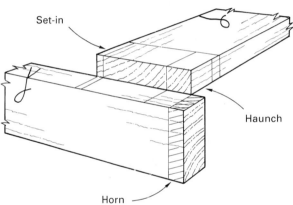

Fig 12.5 Transferring markings from rail to stile.

through, producing a bridle joint, it is stopped some distance from the end, approximately a quarter of the tenon's width. This has reduced the efficiency of the tenon somewhat so to combat any tendency to twist, the tenon is extended in a very short form to form the haunch. Clamp the components together in pairs and mark initially as in Figs 12.4a and 12.4b.

The basic rabbeted frame

This is the construction used to accept a glass panel which will be held in place by putty or a beading, thus making replacement possible (see Fig 12.6). Wood panels too are sometimes held in this way. Details are shown in Fig 12.6. After marking out all of the components, the mortises are chopped before working the rabbets. The front (i.e. outside) shoulder length is as seen. The rear or inside shoulder is advanced to fill the rabbet. Any fine adjustment or correction is best made by planing a shaving from the rabbet rather than nibbling at the front shoulder.

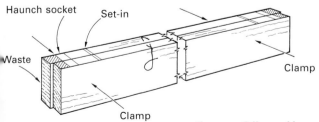

Fig 12.4a Stile markings.

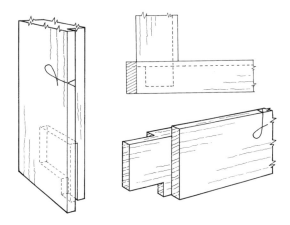

Fig 12.6 Basic rabbeted frame.

The basic grooved frame

This method is used for a grooved-in panel of wood or non-fragile material since replacement is made impossible. It does not permit any decoration other than the stopped chamfer.

The shoulder length is as shown in Fig 12.7. It is customary to make the tenon thickness the same as the groove width, though if it is thicker it presents no problem. Chop the mortise before grooving. The tenon can be sawn before or after, but before is preferable. You will see that on an end view the groove has been nicely filled by the haunch.

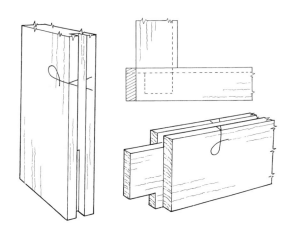

Fig 12.7 Basic grooved frame.

The rabbeted and molded frame

Both shoulders are equal, extending to the bottom of the rabbet (Fig 12.8). Mark out, then chop the mortises and saw the tenons. Next work the molding, and then finally the rabbet. It is greatly convenient if the depth of the rabbet coincides with the depth, i.e., the quirk, of the molding.

Miter the molding on the rails, using the template which is described on page 122. Tap up the joint and mark the start of the miter on the stile. Remove the waste from the molding down to the rabbet level, leaving a little space for the miter. Using the template, pare back the miter to the mark. The joint should now fit.

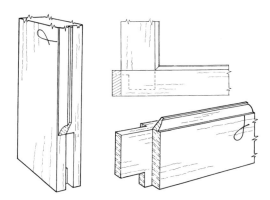

Fig 12.8 Rabbeted and molded frame.

The grooved and molded frame

The shoulder length is measured from the bottom of the molding, which is most convenient if it has a quirk (Fig 12.9). Chop the mortise and saw the tenon. Work the molding, then miter the rails and tap up the joints to mark the miters on the stiles. Remove the waste down to the molding step, then trim back the miters to the mark. It is generally most convenient to polish moldings and inner edges, together with the panels, before the glue-up.

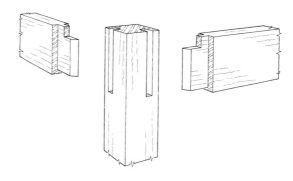

The table or stool construction

This construction is illustrated in Fig 12.10. Mark out the rails in pairs, the long and the short. Clamp the legs together, then offer up a rail and transfer its markings. Ensure that there is some waste to form the horn. Saw the tenons and chop the mortises (refer back to pages 32 and 47 for details of how to do this). Miter the tenon ends.

Fig 12.10a Table or stool construction.

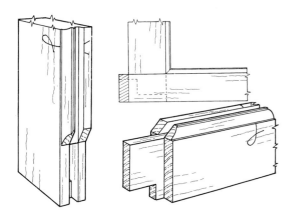

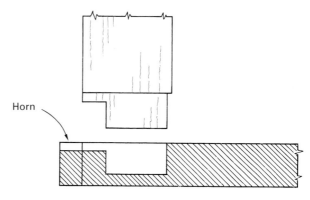

Fig 12.10b Section through leg joint.

Fig 12.9 Grooved and molded frame.

Where the rails are not flush, but set back (see Fig 12.11), mortise gauge the rails first, then adjust the fence to mark the legs. Where a number of such constructions is being made, you can save time by cutting a piece of plywood of the required thickness, boring a hole in it and slipping it over the end of the gauge. Rails would then be marked with the ply in place, and the legs marked with it removed, no fence adjustment being necessary. (For more on mortise and tenon joints, see pages 32 and 47.)

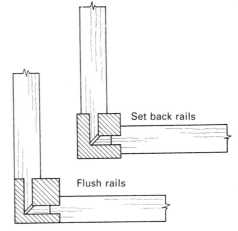

Fig 12.11

Dowel Joints

Chapter 13

There is certainly a place for dowelling, something between a mortised-and-tenoned and a nailed or screwed joint. The original tools for dowelling were the brace and the dowel bit (see Chapter 10). An alternative was the less wieldy twist bit. The dowel shaver bit produced an end bevel on the dowel and is now virtually extinct. These are shown in Fig 13.1. In an emergency, a pencil sharpener will do the trick. Square strips can be malleted through a steel dowel plate to make dowels but the poor quality of the dowel produced, together with the availability of machined dowelling and precut dowels, has rendered the dowel plate, too, virtually obsolete.

The two major modern developments have been the electric hand drill and the lip-and-spur drill, page 82. These are now the generally-used tools. Many varieties of electric drill are also now available with numerous added facilities, none of which are required for simple drilling. Therefore very basic and older models are completely adequate for this work.

Preparation and method

The dowels themselves may be bought preformed in packs or may be cut up from lengths of dowel rod. In both cases, check that both the dowel and the drill have the same sizing, either metric or imperial. The only measurements which for practical purposes correspond identically are 5/16 in. and 8 mm.

Pre-formed dowels are grooved all around to permit the escape of surplus glue. Dowel rods are not grooved in this way. Grooving can easily be achieved either by tapping cut-to-size dowels through

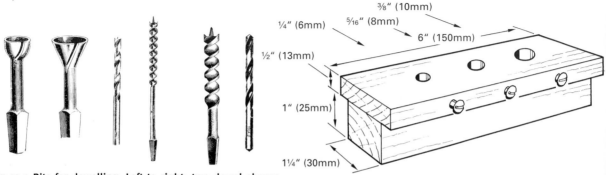

Fig 13.1 Bits for dowelling. Left to right: two dowel shaver bits; lip and spur drill; twist bit; dowel bit and twist drill.

Fig 13.2a Dowel groover.

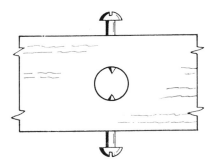

Fig 13.2b Plan detail.

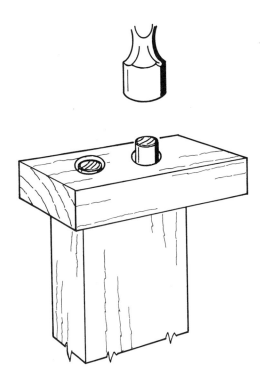

Fig 13.3 Gauging dowels to length.

a workshop-made grooving tool (Fig 13.2) or else by pulling a handled grooving tool along the length of the rod before sawing up. As you will see, two grooves will suffice. Sawn-off dowels need a slight chamfer on each end for easy entrance.

Although dowels are often glued into both components at the same time, it is better to glue first into one only. This method allows an easy dry clamp to check that all is well.

Having glued the dowels into one component first, the correct protrusion can be guaranteed by either of two methods. The first option is to take a block of the correct thickness, drill it oversize, place it over each dowel in turn and tap the dowel flush (Fig 13.3). Alternatively, the block can be slipped over extra-long dowels which are then sawn flush (Fig 13.4).

As quickly as possible, remove all glue which has exuded. A long, narrow strip of wet rag and perhaps an old toothbrush are the tools for this job. Leave the assembly to harden thoroughly before attempting a dry clamp-up – while surface glue hardens rapidly, the glue inside the holes takes much longer.

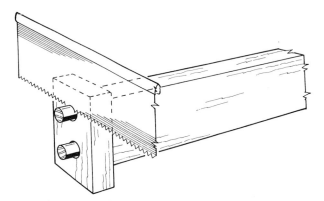

Fig 13.4 Sawing dowels to length.

Edge jointing

Dowels can be used in the edge jointing of boards as an alternative to a loose tongue. Their purpose is not so much to strengthen the joint, since modern adhesives alone are quite adequate, but rather to align two components. Any slight bowing can be controlled. Locating by dowels makes it easy to glue up a number of boards at one clamping.

The two boards are clamped together and the dowel positions squared across both (Fig 13.5). They are then separated and center lines gauged across these marks (Fig 13.6). Gauging must be done from

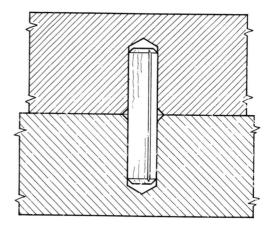

Fig 13.7a Section through a dowel joint.

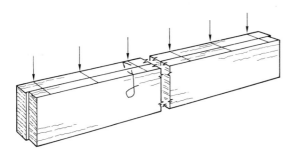

Fig 13.5 Dowel positions marked.

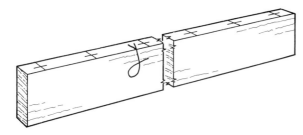

Fig 13.6 Dowel centers gauged.

the true face. The holes can now be bored. They are very slightly countersunk to remove any splinters and to give space for any exuded glue, either of which may prevent a perfect closure of the joint (Fig 13.7). The joint must then be clamped.

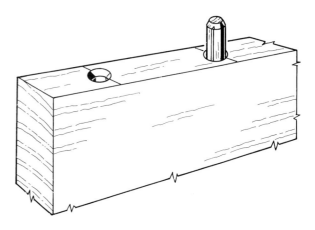

Fig 13.7b Countersunk dowel holes and chamfered and grooved dowel.

Basic flat frames

For flat frames (as in Fig 13.8), the dowel joint is an alternative to the mortise and tenon (see Fig 13.9). The rails need to be cut precisely. The center lines are gauged on all pieces; then the dowel centers are

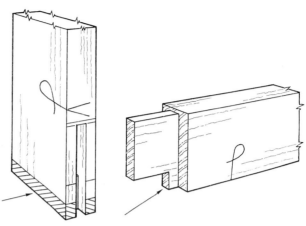

Fig 13.9b Mortise and tenon joint for a flat frame. Dowelling is a simple alternative to this.

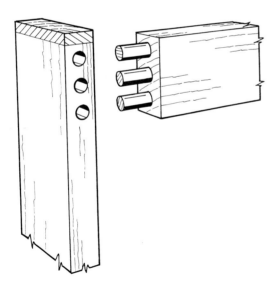

Fig 13.8 The basic flat frame.

can now be drilled, a little deeper than half the dowel length. Countersink slightly; again, this will remove any splinters and provide room for exuded glue, either of which could prevent a perfect fit (Fig 13.7). Glue the dowels into one component and clean off. When the glue is dry, clamp up to test the fit. Glue up the frame.

The surface should require the minimum of cleaning-up. Where there is a muntin, or center rail, this is marked and then offered up to the stile and the centers are taken from it.

Fig 13.9a Dowel joint for a flat frame.

squared across the rail ends. Rails are now offered up to the stiles and the centers are taken off, as in Fig 13.10. Stab the centers with an awl. The holes

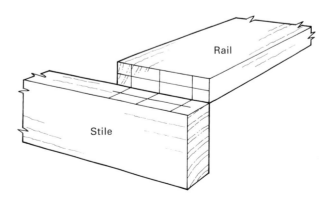

Fig 13.10 Transferring centers from rail to stile.

The load-bearing flat frame

Cut the stiles to length. Cut the rails to the "inside" length plus twice the depth of the housing. Mark the centers and bore in the usual way. Glue the dowels into the rails and clean off any exuded glue. Knock the joints up then scribe the rail width on to the stiles. Cut out the housings. Clamp up again, check the fit and glue in place. Should a rail appear too tight for the housing, plane a few shavings from the rail; this is preferable to nibbling at the housing.

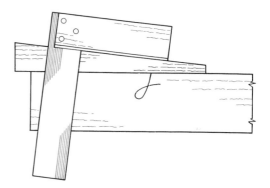

Fig 13.12 Marking the rail shoulders for a tapered frame.

into the rails, then clamp up dry. Test for twist and for equal diagonals, then glue up.

The rabbeted frame

This construction (shown in Fig 13.13) is used to contain a glass panel, mirror or wood panel held in by a pinned beading. It calls for the long and short shoulder construction. The short shoulder is the visible one, i.e. at the front. The long shoulder is needed to fill up the rabbet.

Cut the stiles to length. Prepare the rails (and any muntins) and mark the short shoulder, i.e. the visible length, on the true face. Advance the shoulder on the other side by the depth of the rabbet

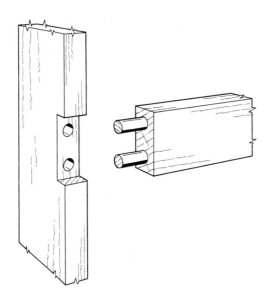

Fig 13.11 A load-bearing flat frame.

The tapered flat frame

First prepare a tapered strip, say 8 in. (200 mm) long and of the same angle of taper as the frame. Use this between the try square and the workpiece (see Fig 13.12). Next, mark out the joints and then bore into the end grain parallel with the edges. Bore into the side grain at the taper angle. Glue the dowels

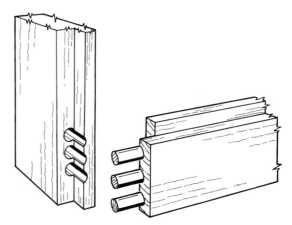

Fig 13.13 Rabbeted frame.

required. This is the long shoulder. Saw off at this point. Gauge the rabbet width and depth on all the components and the rabbet width on the end grain of the rails. Mark the dowel centers and bore in the normal way. Saw off at the short shoulder, producing a step which will fill the rabbet. Glue the dowels into the rail ends.

Work the rabbet either by router, power saw or by hand planing. If the visible short shoulder does not close fully, take a few further shavings from the rabbet. If the inner shoulder shows a slight gap, take a shaving from the lip. Glue up, checking for twist and equal diagonals.

A variation

The following variation, which is shown in Fig 13.14, is sometimes called the cabinet maker's method.

Prepare the components to size, the stiles being naturally the length as seen. The rail length is the visible size plus twice the rabbet depth. Mark out as for the basic frame and bore the holes. Then work

the rabbets. Any molding on the outside would be worked now. In working an ovolo or any stepped molding it is very convenient if the step is cut to the same depth as the rabbet. Glue the dowels into the rails. Miter the ends of the rails, using a mitering template (as described on page 122), then push the frame together. Mark the ends of the miters onto the stiles by holding a square across. Separate and roughly cut the stile miters, at the same time cutting back the lip by stages. When cut back exactly to the bottom of the rabbet, the miter can finally be trimmed exactly.

Clamp the assembly up dry, then check and correct any slight irregularities. Finally, glue up and rapidly remove any surplus glue.

The grooved frame

This construction is used for permanently fixed wood panels and is quite unsuitable for mirrors or glass as breakages cannot be replaced. The grooved frame is illustrated in Fig 13.15.

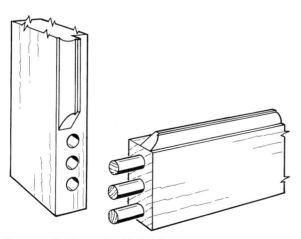

Fig 13.14 Molded and rabbeted frame.

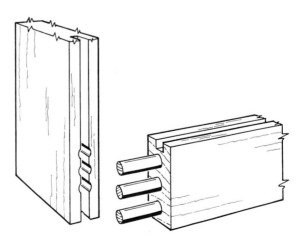

Fig 13.15 Basic grooved frame.

Simple form

Cut all the components to length as seen. Mark out and joint as for the basic flat frame. Dowels can now be glued into the rails and the grooves worked. After a test clamping, the frame can be glued up.

The groove will be visible at the ends of the stiles. This can either be accepted (on temporary or unimportant work), or plugged after the glue-up. This simple form of grooved frame should not be used for top-quality work.

The craftsman's method

This is shown in Fig 13.16. This time, cut the rails longer than seen by twice the depth of the groove. Mark out and bore as for the basic flat frame. Mark the shoulders and cut back to give a stub tenon which fits the groove. This can be easily done. Now glue the dowels into the rails and, when dry, assemble the whole frame. This construction is suitable for a plain undecorated frame or one with chamfers.

The grooved and molded frame

This is shown in Fig 13.17. First, saw the components to size. Stiles are as normal. Rails are measured to the bottom of the groove. Mark out and make the joint as for the basic flat frame. The dowels may be glued into the rails either now or later, as preferred. First work the groove, then the moldings. It is preferable to make the depth of the molding the same as the depth of the groove. With a more complex molding it is probably better to work the molding first. This completed, cut the miters on the ends of the rails, using a sharp chisel and a miter template (page 122).

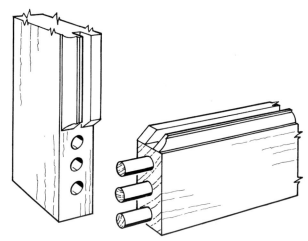

Fig 13.17 Grooved and molded frame.

Now clamp up the frame and mark where the miters will appear on the stile moldings. Remove the waste down to the bottom of the groove and molding. Leave just a little spare near the miter. Cut the stile miters with the template, then clear out the last remnants of the waste.

The frame can now be clamped together and tested for squareness. Depending on the polishing

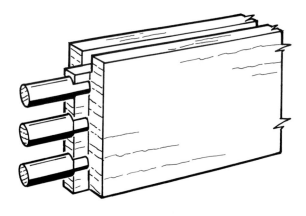

Fig 13.16 Grooved frame, craftsman's method.

method chosen, it is generally recommended that the moldings and inner lips should be polished before the glue-up.

In all cases the ends of the rails should be trimmed on an accurate shooting board. After gluing, test all frames for fit, equal diagonals (i.e., for squareness), and wind (i.e., twisting). All true faces should be out and all true edges inwards.

Table or stool

All components are produced to size and sawn to length. Face and edge marks must be pencilled on clearly. Mark out precisely the dowel centers on one rail and one leg. For flush rails (Fig 13.18a) use the same gauge setting for the leg and the rail. For a set-in rail (Fig 13.18b), the gauge must be re-set after gauging the rails. Proceed normally with the boring.

A convenient arrangement for a set-in of say ⅛ in. (3mm) is to cut out a piece of ⅛ in. (3mm) plywood roughly the size of the gauge fence, bore a hole in it to take the stem and make a slot to pass over the point. With this in place, gauge the rails. Remove and gauge the legs.

Dowel marker pins

These are a re-emergence of a Victorian product (see Fig 13.19). Dowel marker pins seem to be generally available in the standard sizes ¼ in. (6mm), ⁵⁄₁₆ in. (8mm) and ⅜ in. (10mm) although it is possible that larger sizes do exist. They prove particularly useful for carcass work but can, of course, be used for the other joints described.

For frame constructions (note, these have no "horns"), each of the components can be positioned in a simple right-angle jig to be knocked up (Figs 13.20 a and b).

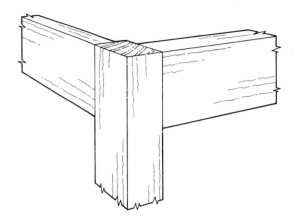

Fig 13.18a Table joint with flush rails.

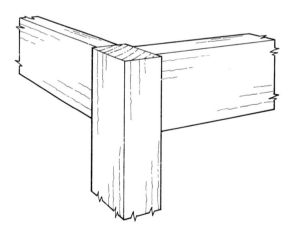

Fig 13.18b Table joint with set-in rails.

Fig 13.19 Dowel marker pin.

Carcass joints

Jointing boards or man-made materials to make cabinets or shelving can also be done by dowelling (Figs 13.21a and b), although this technique has certain limitations. The perfect corner, generally a form of dovetail, cannot be achieved by dowelling. Holes bored very near the end of a board are weak. The top and the base of a cabinet therefore require an upstand or an outstand. In other words, the top or bottom must overhang the sides or else the sides

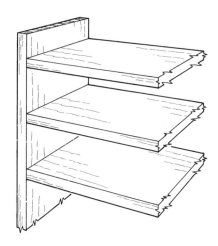

Fig 13.21a A typical carcass jointing.

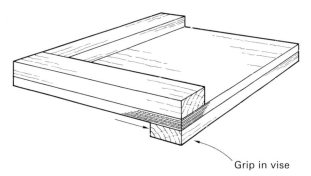

Fig 13.20a Jig for use with marker pins.

Grip in vise

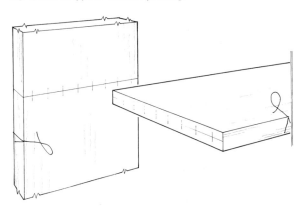

Fig 13.21b Dowel centers only required.

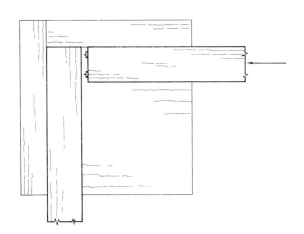

Fig 13.20b Tapping up a flat frame.

must continue above the top and below the bottom. Both methods can be used in the same cabinet, i.e. it can have an overhanging top and downward extended sides. Furthermore, a simple butted dowel joint lacks both elegance and strength, so a housing needs to be incorporated. The housing will support the weight and keep the board flat, but it has no strength. The dowels are the bonding element.

Begin by cutting the housed components, i.e. shelves or partitions, to the sight length plus twice the housing depth. The housing components are cut to the length seen. At this stage it is only necessary

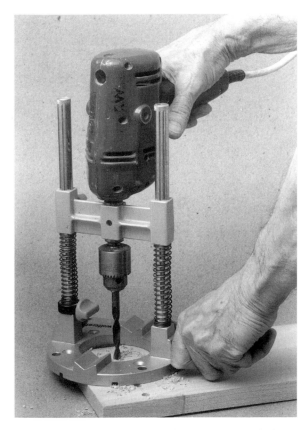

Fig 13.22 A drill attachment which guarantees vertical drilling and a pre-set depth.

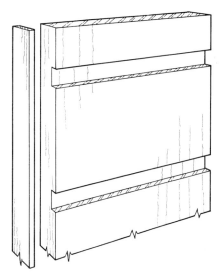

Fig 13.23 Joint concealed by glued-on strips.

to mark the center lines and the dowel centers. The housings are dealt with later.

Drill on these centers as deeply as possible without coming through. A drilling machine, drill stand or vertical drilling attachment (Fig 13.22) helps with precision. Beware of brad point drills with very long points. If necessary, grind off an ordinary twist drill at 90° to finish off a hole at maximum depth.

Now drill the shelf or similar components. Insert, but do not glue in yet, a short dowel in the two outside holes of the shelf and tap the joint together. With a sharp, thin knife, scribe across the two faces of the shelf to mark the precise width of the housing. The housing can now be cut to depth using either a hand or a power router. For the best possible fit, chop down the knife lines with a wide chisel and then remove the waste.

If, as is generally the case, a visible joint is not acceptable, then stop the housing say ½ in. (12 mm) from the front edge and notch the shelf accordingly. Alternatively, work the housing right through then conceal the joint by applying a strip of matching material (Fig 13.23).

Now glue the dowels into the shelf ends. Use a thicknessed, bored block to ensure that the correct length of dowel protrudes. Clean off surplus glue with a long strip of wet rag. Complete any shaping, finishing and polishing of the inside surfaces.

Glue together, using sash clamps or a carcass clamping system. Make sure that the clamping blocks are made to the full width of the job and are slightly curved on the contact faces so as to apply pressure at the center of the joint and not only at the edges. Check for squareness and make sure that there is no twist, then remove any surplus glue promptly. Clean up and finish as you would for any cabinet.

Hinging Doors and Boxes

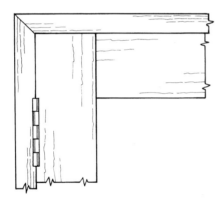

Chapter 14

Fig 14.1 Hinge let in equally to door and carcass. Inelegant.

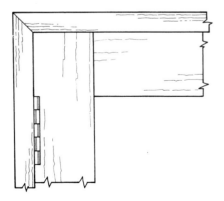

Fig 14.2 Hinge let into door only, preserving the carcass line.

Hinges are applied in two contexts, doors and boxes and are fitted slightly differently in each. Fig 14.1 shows a hinge let into both the door and the carcass (door frame) – the common method of the joiner.

For cabinet work this can be improved on, as it is an inelegant form; the line between the door and the carcass is interrupted by the hinge. A much better technique is to let the hinge completely into the door as in Fig 14.2, thus preserving the line. Doors of veneered plywood and blockboard are often edged with a cocked bead. This can be made to the

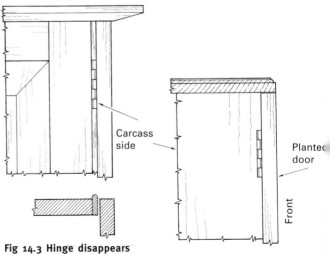

Carcass side

Planted door

Front

Fig 14.3 Hinge disappears optically into a cocked bead.

Fig 14.4 Door planted on front of carcass.

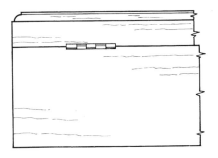

Fig 14.5 Box with sawn-off lid.

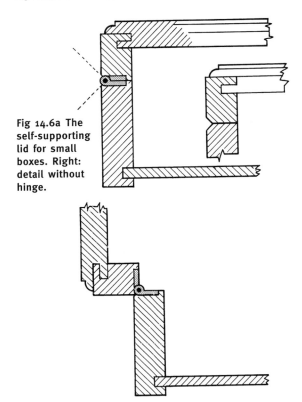

Fig 14.6a The self-supporting lid for small boxes. Right: detail without hinge.

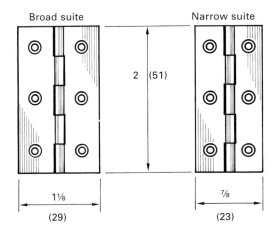

Fig 14.7 Hinge proportions.

Boxes and caskets with "sawn-off" lids (see Fig 14.5) generally have the hinge let equally into the box and the lid. A slight modification, Fig 14.6, will allow a lid to support itself when opened. This arrangement, suitable for small decorative pieces, will not stand much abuse and is therefore unsuitable for larger, heavier items. With planted-on, overhanging lids, it is customary to let the hinge fully into the box, in the manner of the door, as in Fig 14.8.

Fig 14.6b Open position: lid supported by two bevels.

same thickness as the hinge thickness. The hinge then tends to disappear, optically, into the bead. This was a feature of much of the World-War-era "Utility" furniture, as in Fig 14.3. In cases where the door is planted directly on to the front of a carcass as in Fig 14.4, the hinge is let completely into the carcass.

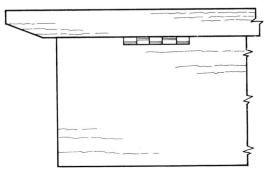

Fig 14.8 Planted on lid.

For the best quality work, solid drawn brass hinges will be used. Check them carefully, file away any irregularities, polish with increasingly fine grades of emery cloth and finish with metal polish. One of the coarser brass polishes is best. Hinges are made in two widths, termed standard and narrow suite. For cheaper work, pressed brass and iron hinges are available. Plastic hinges are increasingly on offer. They are particularly suitable in bathrooms, kitchens and other damp or steamy places. Their effect is lost unless brass- or zinc-plated screws are used. Before actually commencing work, check the following:

1 Are the hinges truly parallel?
2 Are the ends square?
3 Are the screw heads below the surface of the hinge (see Fig 14.9)?

The first two of these faults can be corrected by careful filing and the third by further countersinking. Faults one and two are rare, though three is much more common.

For complete accuracy the marking-out should be done with a marking knife and two gauges, preferably cutting gauges, set with the bevels inwards, i.e. facing the stock. Set one gauge to size A and one to size B, as in Fig 14.10.

On a framed door, position the hinge in line with the inner edge of the rails, as in Fig 14.11. On a flush door, position the top hinge its own length from the top and the lower hinge just a little further up from the bottom to allow for the foreshortening effect if the door is much below eye level, as in Fig 14.12. This will be reversed if the door is well above eye level.

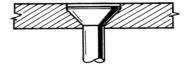

Fig 14.9 Check countersinking on hinge.

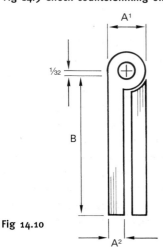

Fig 14.10

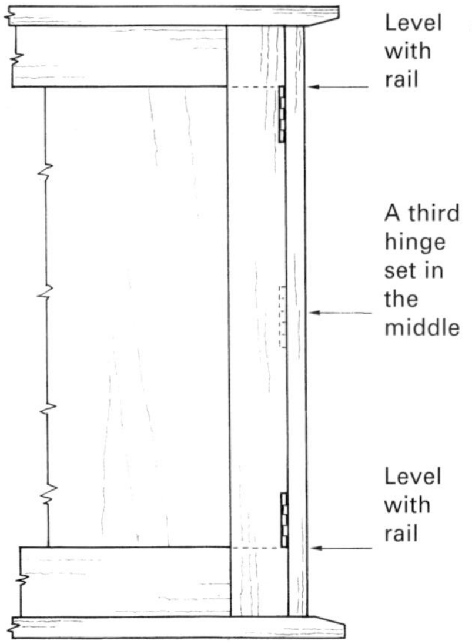

Fig 14.11 Hinge position on a framed door.

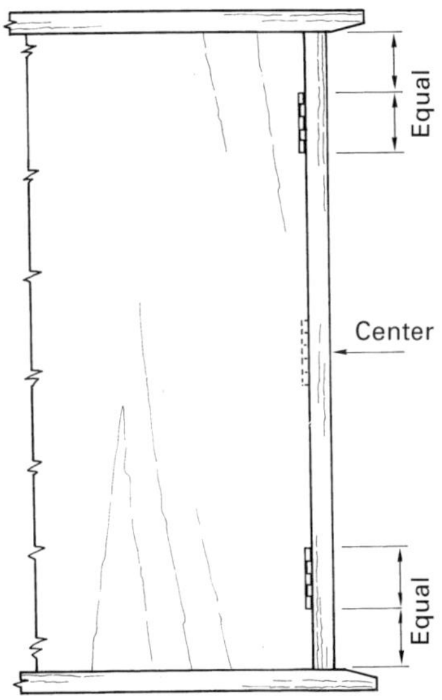

Fig 14.12 Hinge position on a flush door.

Carrying Out the Work

Door in a carcass

Having fitted the door, hold it in its place in the carcass. A tiny wedge under the bottom helps here – it also ensures clearance when opening and closing. Using the hinge itself, inscribe its position on both door and carcass. Proceed to mark out as shown in Fig 14.13. Cut out the sockets as in Fig 14.14. A

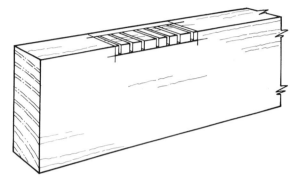

Fig 14.15 Saw cuts help in removal of waste.

number of saw cuts made in the door helps with the removal of waste (Fig 14.15).

Planted on door

The positions of the sockets is reversed here, as shown in Fig 14.16, but the method is the same.

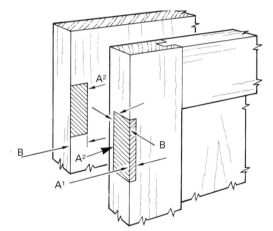

Fig 14.13 Sockets marked out for a door inside the carcass.

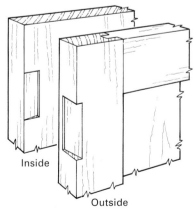

Fig 14.14 Hinge sockets on a set-in door.

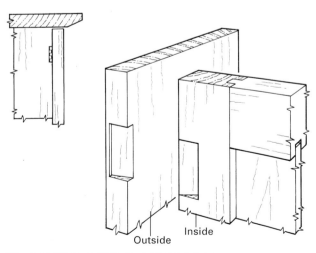

Fig 14.16 Hinge sockets on a planted door.

Boxes

On the sawn-off lid box, the position of the hinges is best marked before the lid is sawn off, but this often tends to be overlooked. Equal sockets are cut; this is quite a straightforward job. On small, fine work a support block should be clamped on to prevent splitting off the thin remaining lip, as in Fig 14.17.

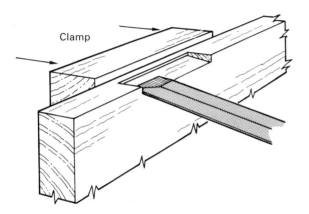

Fig 14.17 Use a support block when lip is thin.

On boxes with overhanging lids, offer up the lid to the back edge and mark the hinge positions. On the box, let in to full thickness. On the lid, square in an adequate distance and then gauge. Chop out the sockets, as in Figs 14.17 & 14.18.

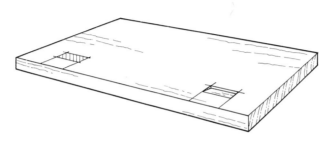

Fig 14.18 Hinge sockets in an overhanging lid.

Faults in hinging

Screw-head interference

Here, the hinge is insufficiently countersunk so the projecting screw heads prevent the door or lid from closing. The remedy is to countersink deeper, as in Fig 14.19.

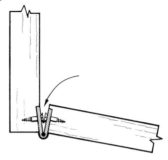

Fig 14.19 Screw-head interference. Heads prevent closing countersink deeper.

Hinge interference

In this case, the sockets have been cut too deep. In closing, the lid or door tries to pull out the screws and will not close (Fig 14.20). The only remedy here is to pack up the hinge sockets with thin strips or pieces of veneer as inconspicuously as possible. Alternatively, carefully cut and glue in a piece of the same wood and start again.

Fig 14.20 Hinge interference. Closing the door tears out screws.

Two refinements

The better quality hinges have five knuckles. It is always customary on the best work to plant the three-knuckle leaf on the larger component, i.e., the carcass or door frame, and the two-knuckle leaf on the smaller component, i.e. the door.

The position of the screw slots can make or mar the appearance of an otherwise well-fitted hinge. Either line up the slots parallel to the hinge pin, or else leave the outer two at right angles to the pin. Fig 14.21 shows these alternatives. Cross-head screws should also be lined up neatly.

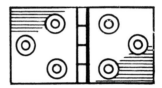

Fig 14.23 Backflap hinge for table leaves without a rule joint.

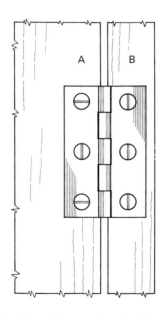

Fig 14.21 Avoid scruffy screw heads. Line up slots as A or B.

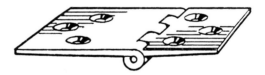

Fig 14.24 Rule joint hinge. Countersinking is on the opposite side to the knuckle.

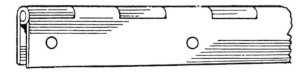

Fig 14.22 Piano strip hinge. These hinges are sold in 6ft. (1,830 mm) lengths, and are usually not let in.

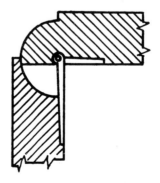

Fig 14.25 Cross-section of a rule joint table.

The Workbench

There can be few subjects upon which woodworkers will disagree more than the workbench. However, for readers with no very definite or strongly held views, the following is suggested as a good general-purpose bench. It is both economical and straightforward in construction as well as being comfortable to work at.

Use mortise-and-tenon joints to fasten the underframing, from 3 x 4 in. wood (or nearest convenient size). Good, clean softwood is quite adequate although hardwood may of course be used at added cost.

The top must be of hardwood of a minimum thickness of 2 in. (50 mm) and as dry as possible.

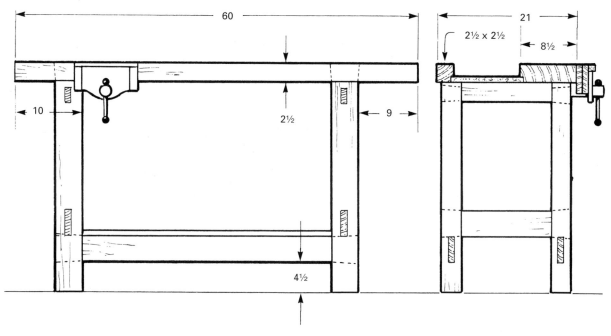

Fig A1.1 A basic workbench. Underframing should be from 2 x 4 nominal wood. A suggested height would be 34 in.

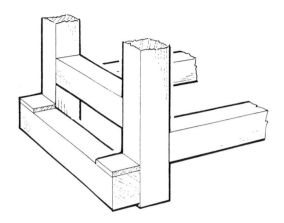

The back rail may be of softwood but must be of an equal thickness. Both these components are rabbeted to accept the well board. The latter should not be softwood, as after a number of years in the dry some softwoods flake. These flakes can easily catch under the fingernails when picking out tools – quite a painful experience. Blockboard, plywood or chipboard are more suitable.

If you cannot obtain a hardwood top, you can make a satisfactory substitute by gluing up a number of layered of multi-ply. Apply solid edges, with a renewable top of hardboard.

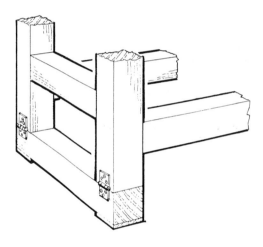

Fig A1.3 A device to raise a bench to suit differing heights of workers.

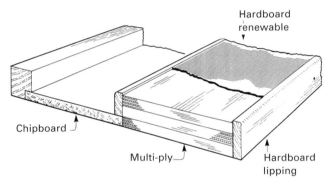

Chipboard

Multi-ply

Hardboard lipping

Hardboard renewable

Fig A1.2 An alternative bench top.

By tenoning through the top and back rail, you can obtain great rigidity without needing an obtrusive long rail at the front which would hinder clamping. Stop short the tenons through the top and back rails, wedge them, then fill in and plane flush. Bolt through near the inner edge to obtain extra security for the top. Similarly, fill the bolt hole. After some months of use, this nut may require tightening.

Board in the lower rails to form a shelf. The more material that is stored here the better, since it gives added solidity to the bench. In a community workshop, where benches are used by woodworkers

of widely differing heights, you may wish to use hinged blocks (Fig A1.3) to give a choice of two heights to the work surface.

The vise, with rabbeted ends and a routing strip, has been described previously (see page 76). Left-handers will, of course, need to fit their vises on the right-hand end of the bench. The following holding system is most strongly recommended.

Use a tail vise with the customary wooden jaws. Fit the moving jaw with one which is extra thick. Groove this to take a sliding hardwood dog. Tap the metal jaw to take a thumbscrew. A sheet metal clip protects the dog from the screw. Quite a light, cheap vise can be adapted for the purpose. A new vise, fitted by the makers with a sliding metal dog, is both heavy and expensive.

A recent development on these lines has been the introduction by Record of a combined light tail vise and planing grip at quite an economical price. This should work well with the system described,

Groove the bench edges and fit each side with a metal strip of ⅛ x 3 in. (3 x 20 mm). In addition to the countersunk holes for the screws, drill the strip ¼ in. (6 mm) at regular intervals. This spacing must be comfortably less than the amount of move-

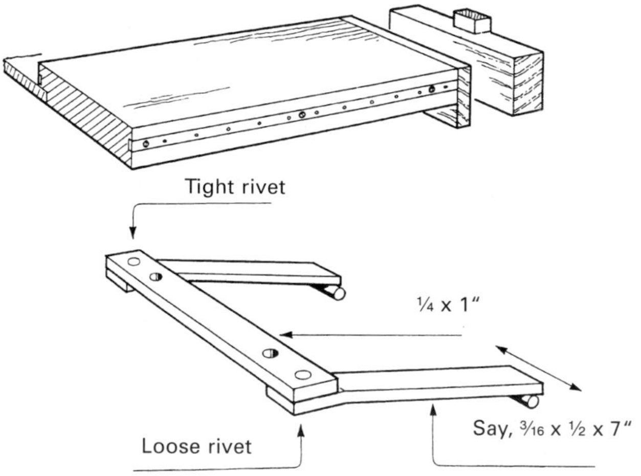

Fig A1.4 A holding device for planing, etc.

ment of the tail vise. Rivet two cranked arms to the planing stop bar; the inner one should be hammered tight and rigid, while the outer one should be less so, allowing a small amount of tight rotation. Braze or silver solder short ¼ in. (6 mm) steel pegs to the

ends. These should fit comfortably into the steel strips. Before finally screwing fast the steel strips, it is important to check that the stop bar is quite square to the bench front.

The stop bar can be drilled and countersunk underneath to permit the attachment of shaped wood blocks to hold curved, circular or irregularly shaped pieces. Thick components are catered for by inserting a wood block under the stop bar.

Two drawers hung from the bench top are handy for small tools and accessories. They must be close to the bench edge, say 6 in. (152 mm), to permit clamps and handscrews to be used.

A useful holdfast of the type illustrated in

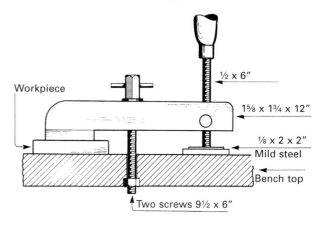

Fig A1.5 Suggested sizes for a bench holdfast.

Drill three or four ½ in. (13 mm) holes through the bench top, counterbore underneath and force a ½ in. hex nut into each. Make the clamping and tensioning screws with threaded rod.

Shooting Boards

The 90° shooting board and the miter shooting board are a considerable improvement on the conventional models in that the stop block cannot be worn by misuse, causing tear-out, and the plane cannot be held at a wrong angle. They are both left- and right-handed so that components which have a molded corner can always be planed into the molding, again avoiding tear-out. Sizes are only suggestions. Very small shooting boards accepting a block plane are useful for fine work.

The 90° shooting board

The multi-ply base has a runner made from acrylic sheet screwed on to it. Offcuts of this sheet may be obtained from makers of illuminated signs.

Alternatively, two thicknesses of plastic laminate, such as Formica, may be glued together. A gripping strip for the vise is screwed and glued to the lower face.

Make two end blocks from hardwood to suit the plane width. Cut out the two front corners to accept the runners. Work two ¼ in. (6 mm) slots in the block to take screws. Now glue and screw the end blocks to the base. To check that they are square to the runner it is best to use a large draftsman's set-square and hold a block tightly against the runner. This is more accurate than the average workshop try square.

Prepare a top rail from sound, dry hardwood and similarly screw the upper runner to it. This should project about 1⁄16 in. (2 mm). Then screw the

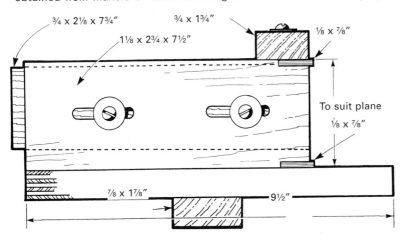

¾ x 2⅛ x 7¾"   ¾ x 1¾"
1⅛ x 2¾ x 7½"   ⅛ x ⅞"
To suit plane
⅛ x ⅞"
⅞ x 1⅞"   9½"

Fig A2.1 90° shooting board, end view.

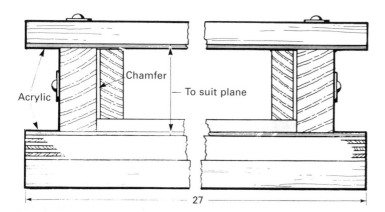

Fig A2.2 90° shooting board, side view.

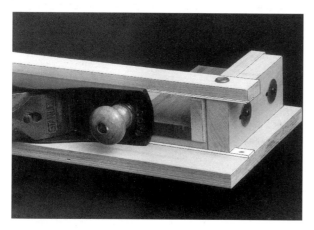

Fig A2.3 Method of use, showing workpiece and thrust block.

rail in place with a No. 10 or 12 roundhead screw and a large diameter washer. This operates through a slightly elongated hole to allow slight adjustment, hence this joint is not glued. Make a loose platform from ½ in. (12 mm) multi-ply or MDF (medium density fiberboard) to fit between the end blocks, and rabbet it to fit over the runner. Secure with a few well-countersunk screws.

Now test for accuracy as follows. Saw off the corner from a small plastic try square until it will freely pass under the top rail. Hold a plane firmly against the two runners and check for 90° between the plane and platform, adjusting the top rail as necessary. Make the thrust blocks to fit against the end blocks with a sliding fit. Secure with No. 10 or 12 roundhead woodscrews and large washers.

Hold the plane firmly in place and test that the thrust blocks are square to it with the large set square. If accurately prepared they should still be square but, if they are not, correct by careful planing. Move the thrust blocks just forward of the runners and screw up firmly. Then plane with a fine cut until the plane will cut no more. If the thrust blocks do become worn, advance them then again plane until the plane ceases to cut. The blade must always be kept very sharp. It is wise to keep a special blade for shooting board work, ground and sharpened completely square. A hanging hole will help reduce knocks which could render the board inaccurate.

For planing miters, as for example on picture frames, a 45° block can be added when required. This must be made from glued-together layers of multi-ply since solid wood may shrink, rendering the angle incorrect. Again, roundhead screws with large washers are preferable, passing through short slots which will allow adjustment for wear. With a 45° set square check the angels between block and plane sole. There is no problem of tear-out when cutting wood at 45°, hence no thrust blocks are needed.

The miter shooting board

This has a similar baseboard, but its gripping bar is underneath. Cut a groove of ¼ x ¼ in. (6 x 6 mm) near one edge and screw the two lower runners on, after angling them at 45°.

Make the end blocks, this time by building up from layers of multi-ply to avoid shrinkage, which would decrease the 45° angle. Cut one end of each at 45°, saw notches to take the runners and cut the screw slots. Screw on the end blocks but do not glue. Check for squareness with the outer runner. Fit the top runner to the top rail then screw this in place with No. 10 or 12 screws and washers through an elongated hole.

Add the loose platform and the thrust blocks, then test for accuracy. Hold a plane firmly against the

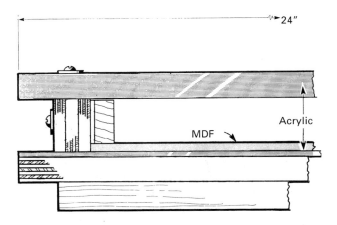

Fig A2.5 45° shooting board, side view.

runners and check for squareness of the end blocks with a large set square. If all is well, unscrew the end blocks, glue with a slower-setting glue, then re-screw them. Having quickly returned the top rail, check again for 45° between the platform and the plane sole.

Replace the thrust blocks, checking again for squareness. If they are not quite square, adjust by gently planing. On both shooting boards, the outer end of the thrust blocks should be chamfered to prevent splitting off.

A refinement you might consider is securing the top rails more firmly by using a cylindrical nut with a machine screw and washer in place of the large woodscrew. On the 90° board the top rail may be rabbeted for the runner.

Acrylic sheets can be planed and sawn either by hand or machine. The runners are best planed screwed to a board.

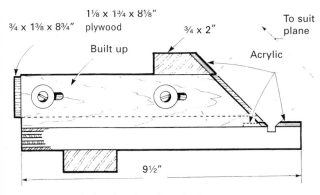

Fig A2.4 45° shooting board, end view.

Two Useful Workshop Templates

After a long gap, these two templates are again commercially available for use in the workshop. However, many readers will feel that they cannot justify the expense of these templates for the amount of use expected. Successful all-wood models can easily be made (see Figs A3.1 and A3.2), as they were in former times.

Almost any hardwood may be used, but I consider actual hardness to be more important than the particular species. If green wood is used, shrinkage will naturally take place and this will reduce the miter angle to less than 45°.

First, produce sufficient material to thickness, which will make either one or both templates. Cut

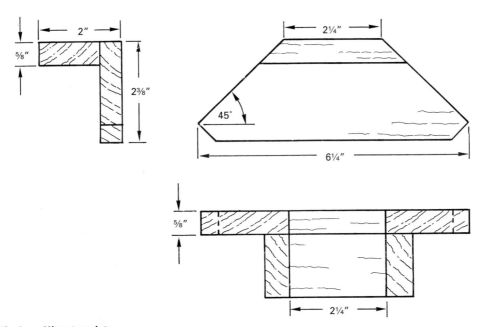

Fig A3.1 Miter template.

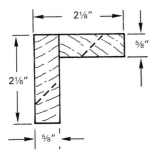

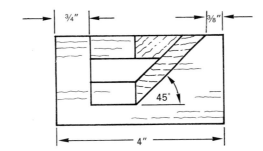

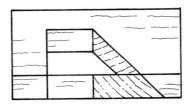

Fig A3.2 Stopped chamfer template.

it into lengths a little longer than the finished size, then glue together. Two things must be carefully watched. Firstly, all traces of glue must be removed from the inside corner, and secondly, the corner angle must be checked to an accurate 90°. When the glue has dried, the assemblies can be gauged exactly and planed to width.

Mark out the details of the angled surfaces with a knife and a gauge, taking great care. Either use the 45° facility of a combination square, or stand the workpiece on a truly flat surface and use a 45° set square. I am suspicious of the accuracy of a prior set sliding bevel. Saw off the waste close to the lines, then finish the outside angles by planing and the inside angle by careful paring with a very sharp chisel, which must be wider than the thickness of the material. The outside ends may be finished on a

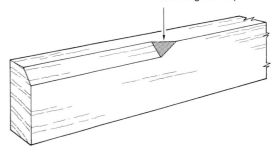

Flat angled stop

Fig A3.3 The stopped chamfer.

disc sander. If this is done carefully, the ends of the stopped chamfer template can be used as a useful small square.

In use always choose a wide chisel, making sure that it sits truly flat on the face of the template. The slightest raising of the handle will cause a cut in the template. Clamp the template to the workpiece. Well made, these templates will outlast their maker.

Gluing Up

Woodworking adhesives

Hide glue

This comes in cake, bead, pearl and ground forms. It is soaked overnight in water then warmed in a glue-pot with a water jacket. Boiling and repeated reheating reduce the efficiency of this glue. When heated, it should run easily off the glue brush. Apply it warm, on to components previously warmed. Speed is of the essence, so thorough preparation of brushes, clamps, blocks and assistants is vital. Joints must be positioned and clamps applied before the glue chills. Any clamping blocks to be used should be waxed on the contact surface to prevent them sticking to the work.

Less common is a liquid form of hide glue which only needs gentle warming. Being soluble in water these glues are not waterproof so should not be used in damp conditions. Clamps should stay on for at least 12 hours. Hide glue is still the most commonly used for veneering by hand methods.

Hot-melt glue

This form of adhesive makes veneering particularly easy. It is simply positioned between the veneer and the ground. Heat can be applied with an ordinary domestic iron, though a specialist iron is available, The method is quick, clean and permanent. Although the material is not cheap, there is literally no waste. Every scrap can be used. Professionally this is a great saving in waiting time. Hot-melt glue is quite impossible to use for any conventional jointing.

The glue gun

If you have a glue gun you can apply hot-melt glue in stick form. You heat the glue in the small electric glue gun and apply the glue to the work through the nozzle. Cooling times are between two and 45 seconds, hence it is unsuitable for clamped joints. The glue line is thicker than is normally accepted for cabinet work. It is handy for small repairs where the components are hand held while the glue sets. It also serves a useful purpose in temporary gluing.

PVA glues

Polyvinyl acetate glues are some of the most recent, popular and widely used glues. They come ready for use and have a relatively long life in the bottle. Clamps can generally be removed after two or three hours. Overnight hardening is recommended before any stress is put on the joint or there is heavy machining. Surplus glue can be washed off easily. In general these glues are not waterproof.

Synthetic resin glues

These glues consist obviously of a synthetic resin and a hardener, usually formic acid. There are two types, one with a separate hardener and one that is combined with a hardener. With the former, the resin may come as a liquid or, for a longer shelf life, as a powder to be mixed with water as required. Resin is applied to one part of the joint and hardener to the other. This is a very clean glue, with little waste, popular in industry. In the combined form both resin and hardener have been dehydrated and the powders mixed together. The addition of water activates the glue. Assembly times are short as are minimum clamping times.

Epoxy resin glues

An expensive glue sold in two tubes – resin and hardener. Equal amounts of these must be mixed. Such glue will bond wood, metal, glass, ceramics and leather, etc. It is of little use to the woodworker except in an emergency although it is suitable for filling gaps and the bond is extremely strong. Make sure that surplus glue is removed immediately.

Super glues

These are expensive and of little use for woodwork. They are handy only for emergency repairs. Keep them off the skin as the bond can be permanent.

Contact adhesives

These rubber-based thixotropic glues, much publicized in the do-it-yourself world, are unsuitable for woodwork though useful for fixing plastic laminates onto worktops.

After the glue-up

Of course, the best way to remove glue is not to let it get there at all. Several methods of prevention can be used. Glue which overspills onto a surface which is later to be planed or trimmed doesn't matter. Glue on a finished surface is the problem.

A wax finish is one solution. Take, for example, a box or a carcass. Protect the joints during polishing with plastic tape and clamp up the job dry for the checking. At this stage run a little extra wax into the corners but do not polish off. After hardening overnight the glue will flake off easily, perhaps just needing the corner of a sharp chisel to start it off.

Other polishes unfortunately give adhesion to the glue, so further protection is needed. Before assembly, position pieces of plastic tape right up to the corners of both parts of the joint. This is better than using masking tape, where the wrinkled surface can allow the glue to creep under it. When the glue has hardened, both glue and tape can be peeled off.

In cases where this is not applicable, the glue must be washed off. Bearing in mind that synthetic resin glue manufacturers give an assembly time of about 10 minutes, and that hide glue chills very rapidly, speed is of the essence. Time will be used up in positioning the clamps and blocks, measuring diagonals and checking for twist, so all equipment including a plastic bowl of hot water with a touch of detergent, a wet rag, one or two absorbent dry rags (all of cotton, not synthetics), a few wooden "chisels" with sharp edges and some old newspapers must be close at hand. An oldish kitchen washing-up bowl (rectangular, not round), an old stubby paintbrush and an old toothbrush are also useful.

As soon as the glue-up is complete, scrape off the excess glue with the wooden chisel, wiping it frequently on the newspaper. Wet one of the brushes well and scrub into the corners, removing the last traces there. Finish with the wrung-out wet rag, then thoroughly dry the work.

If the inside surfaces have been treated with, say, polyurethane varnish, this is the end of the task. But if the surface is untreated, then inevitably the grain will be raised. The quicker the work is dried off, the less this will apply, but in any case, the surface will need rubbing over with fine-grade sandpaper when it is completely dry, and not before.

A final warning. Throw away all rags as they may contain lumps of hardened glue, which can inflict deep scratches on the surface. Similarly, wash out very carefully any brushes which have been used.

Index